THE CREATION OF THE PRESIDENCY
1775-1789

THE CREATION OF THE PRESIDENCY
1775-1789

A Study in Constitutional History

By Charles C. Thach, Jr.

DA CAPO PRESS • NEW YORK • 1969

A Da Capo Press Reprint Edition

This Da Capo Press edition of *The Creation of the Presidency,
1775-1789*, is an unabridged republication of the first edition published in 1922 as Series XL, Number 4, of the *Johns Hopkins
University Studies in Historical and Political Science*.

Library of Congress Catalog Card Number 74-87710

Published by Da Capo Press
A Division of Plenum Publishing Corporation
227 West 17th Street
New York, N. Y. 10011

THE CREATION OF THE PRESIDENCY, 1775-1789

A STUDY IN CONSTITUTIONAL HISTORY

THE CREATION OF THE PRESIDENCY
1775-1789
A Study in Constitutional History

BY

CHARLES C. THACH, Jr., Ph.D.

Instructor in History and Political Science

BALTIMORE

THE JOHNS HOPKINS PRESS

1922

PRESS OF
THE NEW ERA PRINTING COMPANY
LANCASTER, PA.

To the Memory of my Father
CHARLES COLEMAN THACH

CONTENTS

PREFACE

An eminent political scientist has been heard to remark that, while all political scientists necessarily know some history, there are but few historians who know political science. The writer of the present study has little hope of upsetting the judgment. But he does claim that the political scientist has kept the office of the presidency of the United States too exclusively within the sphere of his investigations, whereby an organic institution has been too much considered as a mere catalogue of powers. Were it not for that peculiar relation between the executive and the judicial departments which has made the latter very chary of undertaking to say authoritatively what the presidency is and what it is not, this criticism would not be valid. The history of national executive power might then be read in the Supreme Court Reports. But, in the absence of an authority to speak with finality on many vital matters, such, for example, as the nature of the vesting clause, it has been left to the shifting forces of politics to determine the nature of the office. What could be a more proper sphere for historical investigation?

A further result of this state of things is an enhancement of interest in origins of the office. Lacking authoritative dicta, we may well seek for enlightenment concerning what the presidency is in an analysis of what the presidency was intended to be. And surely, in any event, the history of an institution which has given its name to one of the two great classes of solutions worked out for the problem of popular government is a matter of interest and importance, and the more since it is indeed the oldest executive department in the world in point of view of constitutional existence.

It has been necessary in the course of this study to pass judgment on points that have been, and are, matters subject to vigorously disagreeing interpretation. Indeed, it has been necessary to defend the view of one political party against that of another. Under such circumstances a mere disclaimer of bias may not carry much weight. But it can be said with entire truthfulness that the writer brought one set of opinions to his investigation and came away with another. Nor does he doubt that the future will disclose, as the past has disclosed, more than one complete reversal of position on the part of those in whom consistency seems sometimes not only the rarest, but also the least of all virtues, the leaders of the political parties.

The writer has disclaimed a hope to modify the view of the historian's knowledge of political science cited above. He fears, indeed, that he has but strengthened it. If there are, however, any glimmerings of light, the credit is due to the political scientist in question, Professor W. W. Willoughby. The credit for the darkness is the writer's own.

It is impossible for the graduate student to put into words the debt which he owes to those who have served as his guides in the tangled thickets of history and historical investigation. None but another student, past or present, can appreciate the extent of the debt. For him words are unnecessary. Suffice it to say that if the historical method of the present study be in any degree sound, if there are any, even faint, indications of the utilization of historical judgment and historical imagination, it is to be attributed to those who have taught, both by precept and by example, the writer what of these he was capable of acquiring, Professor J. H. Latané and Professor J. M. Vincent.

The writer wishes further to acknowledge his indebtedness to the monumental work of Professor Farrand, whose scholastic unselfishness in making available for the American student the results of his patient and skillful collection of material relative to the making of the Constitution has in a very real sense made this study a possibility.

In the preparation of the manuscript, the assistance of Miss M. C. Stokes has been invaluable.

The writer cannot close his preface without mention of those whose sacrifices made his graduate work a possibility, whose sympathetic interest made it a pleasure, his father and his mother. It had been his hope to dedicate this study to them, to whom scholastic merit would not be the only interest. It now is a high, though sad, privilege to dedicate it to the memory of his father and of his life spent in the service of the youth of the South.

C. C. T., Jr.

THE CREATION OF THE PRESIDENCY, 1775-1789: A STUDY IN CONSTITUTIONAL HISTORY

CHAPTER I

General Political Tendencies, 1776–1787

It has been said that "the one great problem which every politically organized people has to solve is to establish and maintain a form of government which will be strong enough to perform the duties which are laid upon it and yet so organized that those who obtain the possession of its powers should not be disposed, or, if so disposed, should not be able, to use that authority which they have to advance their own selfish interests in disregard of, or contrary to, the welfare of the governed."[1]

The ascertainment of the point of view from which this central problem of the balance between governmental strength and individual liberty and security is approached is a primary requisite for a true understanding of the work of any given body of constitution makers. The Constitution of the United States is no exception to this general truth, nor to the equally valid historical maxim that "ideal constructions are doubtless the psychic precipitates of social experience."[2]

It is consequently necessary, by way of introduction to the present study, to consider briefly the recent social experiences of the men who slowly gathered in Philadelphia in 1787, in order to obtain an insight into that political psychology which so profoundly influenced the finished instrument of government which was to be submitted to an anxious country four

---

[1] W. W. Willoughby, unpublished MS.
[2] C. L. Becker, Beginnings of the American People, p. 83.

months later.[3] It will be understood, of course, that we are concerned with the political psychology of a relatively limited class. There can be no doubt that the constitutional history of the United States begins with the establishment of the " government of the masses by the classes," [4] and especially that class " denominated 'gentlemen,' who, by reason of their wealth, their talents, their education, their families, or the offices they hold, aspire[d] to a preëminence which the people refuse[d] to grant them," as a disinterested French observer described it.[5]

Within that class there were variations, to be sure. Not all its members reacted in the same fashion to their social experiences. Their differences in this respect explain, indeed, much of the history of the making of the Constitution. But for the present, while the object is to determine general tendencies, it will be proper to consider this gentry, either ruling or seeking to rule, as a whole.

At the beginning of independent American political life these leaders were primarily revolutionists, conservatives at heart, but in rebellion against constituted political authority. As a consequence, the emphasis of their political thought was laid on the element of liberty and political security. Government, as manifested in Great Britain's system of imperial control, had proved an evil. Consequently, it was easy for the men of 1776 to accept the principle that the best of governments was but a necessary evil. Their position forced them to seek for a theoretical justification of the principle of revolution, and they found it in the doctrines of natural

---

[3] The most complete and satisfactory study of this period remains Bancroft, History of the Formation of the Constitution of the United States. Channing's History of the United States, vol. iii, chaps. xiii-xvi, is especially valuable on economic conditions. C. A. Beard, Supreme Court and the Constitution and Economic Interpretation of the Constitution, are valuable and suggestive, especially the former. The latter suffers from over-emphasis of the direct pecuniary interest of the Framers in the redemption of the certificates. H. J. Ford, Rise and Growth of American Politics, is a stimulating study.

[4] H. J. Ford, Rise and Growth, p. 59.

[5] Otto to Vergennes, Oct. 10, 1786; Bancroft, History of the Formation of the Constitution of the United States, vol. i, p. 399.

rights, the contractual origin of government, the consent of the governed and the right of resistance.[6]

Immediately, however, they were subjected to another force, the necessity of conducting a war. But the efficient conduct of war demands a theory of government diametrically opposed to those just mentioned, one whose chief tenet is rather the necessity of governmental energy and of obedience of individuals to governmental mandates. The conduct of war entails, whether rightly or wrongly, an abridgment of personal liberty, a subordination of the security of individuals against government to the dominant purpose of bringing the war to a successful issue. Military considerations tend to dominate civil. The final result, which, when not reached, is at least tended towards, is the dictator who shall see to it that the state suffer no harm.

To this principle the war of the Revolution was no exception. The patriot cause was saved time and time again by the patience and resourcefulness of a single man. American successes flowed from governmental and military vigor, and this vigor came from the exercise of power. On the contrary, American difficulties, of which there were myriads, and American reverses flowed from lack of power.

The conflict of these two sets of principles is apparent throughout the war. On the one hand, there is a struggle for extending government power, conducted by an increasingly influential group of politicians. On the other, there are the efforts of the adherents to the older doctrines to retain the principles of " liberty." [7] The result is a modification of the older views, a gain in importance of the element of authority. The concrete gains of the " authority " school were small. But their failure to achieve anything more substantial strengthened their position. Had government in fact been able to control the individual, to make itself

---

[6] C. E. Merriam, History of American Political Theories, chap. ii. This is the standard authority on general political theory for both the colonial and the early constitutional period.

[7] F. Wharton, Revolutionary Diplomatic Correspondence of the United States, vol. i, p. 252 ff.

felt throughout the continent, there would very probably have been a reaction.   But the cessation of war marked a collapse of government, and found some of the leaders ready even to seek a solution in an appeal to the military powers of the commander-in-chief.[8]

Events subsequent to the war contributed no less strongly than the war itself to heighten the importance of the authority factor in the governmental problem.   The overshadowing fact in governmental history was the complete inability of the government set up by the Articles of Confederation to function.   Efforts to patch up the system were thwarted, once by Rhode Island, again by New York.   It was easily seen that its fundamental defect was the lack of coercive power.   As John Jay somewhat satirically told the people of New York, the framers of the first body of fundamental national law seemed "not to have been sensible that mere advice is a sad substitute for laws; nor to have recollected that the advice of the all wise and best of Beings has been always disregarded by a great majority of all the men that ever lived."[9]

But of far more importance than this abstract governmental fact were the social forces that brought home in a number of very inconvenient ways to the minds of the gentry the truth that governmental strength, and especially national governmental strength, was desirable.   Washington described the situation accurately when he wrote:

> The truth is, the people must *feel* before they will *see;* consequently they are brought slowly into measures of public utility.   Past experiences, or the admonition of a few, have but little weight.[10]

The most important of these practical influences which were operative during the six uneasy years following the termination of actual hostilities were the non-payment of the

[8] The so-called Newburgh conspiracy.   See Gouverneur Morris to Jay, Jan. 1783; Jared Sparks, Life of Gouverneur Morris, vol. i, p. 289.   Quoted in Bancroft, Formation of the Constitution, vol. i, p. 87.
[9] John Jay, "Address to the People of the State of New York, on the subject of the Constitution, By a Citizen of New York," in P. L. Ford, Pamphlets on the Constitution of the United States, p. 72.
[10] John Marshall, Life of George Washington, vol. v, p. 79.

national debt, the general commercial depression and the rising discontent of the poorer classes, which threatened the political control of the gentry, manifested itself in legal tender and stay laws, and, when denied a legal outlet, precipitated disturbances such as those in Connecticut, New Hampshire and, especially, Massachusetts.

It is not within the scope of the present study to trace the history of these events. Their relation to the contemporary view of the problem of government is, however, of evident significance. The payment of the debt required a government strong enough to levy and collect taxes. Lack of authority in Congress to pass retaliatory commercial measures against British trade was, rightly or wrongly, believed fatal to the restoration of commercial prosperity. Laws violating the obligation of contracts could be curbed only by a national organization properly equipped with power for the purpose. Insurrectionary movements, too strong for the individual States to quell, must be put down by the strong arm of a national armed force.

The following description of the political situation is a striking example of the point of view of a representative member of the political upper class, John Marshall:

Two great parties were formed in every state, which were distinctly marked, and pursued distinct objects, with systematic arrangement. The one struggled with unabated zeal for the exact observance of public and private engagements. By those belonging to it the faith of a nation, as of a private man was deemed a sacred pledge, the violation of which was equally forbidden by the principles of moral justice, and of sound policy. The distresses of individuals were, they thought, to be alleviated only by industry and frugality, not by a relaxation of the laws or of a sacrifice of the rights of others. According to the stern principles laid down for their government, the imprudent and idle could not be protected by the legislature from the consequences of their indiscretion; but should be restrained from involving themselves in difficulties by the conviction that a rigid compliance with contracts would be enforced. They were consequently the uniform friends of a regular administration of justice, and of a vigorous course of taxation which would enable the state to comply with its engagements. By a natural association of ideas, they were also, with very few exceptions, in favour of enlarging the powers of the federal government, and of enabling it to protect the dignity and character of the nation abroad, and its interests at home. The other party marked out for itself a more indulgent course. Viewing with extreme tenderness the case of the debtor, their efforts were unceasingly directed to his relief. To exact a faithful compliance with contracts was, in their opinion, a measure too harsh to be insisted upon, and was one which the people would not bear. They were uniformly in favor of relaxing the administration of justice, of affording facilities for the payment of debts, and of suspending their collection, and of remitting taxes. The same course of opinion led them to resist every attempt to transfer from their own hands into those of Congress, powers which by others were deemed essential to the preservation of the union." [11]

Opposition to "relaxation of laws," advocacy of "a rigid compliance with contracts," of "a regular administration of justice," of "enlarging the powers of the federal government," by such principles were the old revolutionary catchwords replaced. There was now no occasion for an appeal to the inalienable rights of man, to equality, to the philosophy of John Locke in general.

How could this be otherwise at a time when the Massachusetts troubles dominated the political thought of the country, events, too, which seemed to portend the most direfully momentous consequences? The letters of the conservative leaders written during the autumn of 1786 are filled with speculations and fears aroused by these transactions. Nothing could better illustrate the conservative state of mind which produced the Constitution than a few excerpts from these letters which shuttled back and forth as the news spread from New England to the country at large:

"The disturbances in Massachusetts," Grayson reported to Monroe from New York, "have been considerable and absolutely threaten the most serious consequences. It is supposed that insurgents are encouraged by emissaries of a certain nation, and that Vermont is in the association. How it will end, God only knows; the present prospects are, no doubt, extremely alarming." [12]

"Dissatisfaction and uneasiness prevail throughout the country," an English observer wrote to his government, "the greater part of the people poor, and many in desperate cir-

---

[11] Ibid., p. 85.
[12] Grayson to Monroe, Nov. 22, 1756; Bancroft, vol. i, p. 405.

cumstances do not, it seems, want any government at all, but had rather have all power and property reduced to a level." [13]

"We learn," so Madison wrote to his father, "that great commotions are prevailing in Massachusetts. An appeal to the Sword is exceedingly dreaded. The discontented, it is said, are as numerous as the friends of Government, and more decided in their measures. Should they get uppermost it is uncertain what may be their effort. They profess to aim only at a reform of their Constitution, and of certain abuses in the public administration; but an abolition of debts, public and private, and a new division of property, are strongly suspected to be in contemplation." [14]

"The troubles in Massachusetts still continue," a correspondent of Washington's reported, "Government is prostrated in the West. And it is much to be feared that there is not enough energy in that State to reestablish the civil powers. The leaders of the mob, whose fortunes and measures are desperate, are strengthening themselves daily; and it is expected that they will soon take possession of the Continental magazine at Springfield, in which there are from ten to fifteen thousand stands of arms, in excellent order." [15]

Rufus King confided his fears to Elbridge Gerry as follows:

Be assured that neither you nor I comprehend the combination which these insurgents may in possible events be able to form. Let them shew their condition and numbers and advance a little further in open resistance of the Government, and a scene will then present itself of far more importance than had yet been conjectured.

There will not be wanting leaders of name and consideration to conduct them. We all have our preferences and aversions, and perhaps in general they are both alike unfounded. I confess, however, that with the single exception of one French nobleman, I have always been more willing to confide in the citizens of our Country, novel as their employments have been, than in the most plausible, or experienced Foreigners who have been among us. Although in some instances we may have received benefits from Foreigners in the public service, yet I have rejoiced when the obligation has been discharged and they have quitted America.

---

[13] Temple to Carmarthen, Oct. 4, 1786; Bancroft, vol. i, p. 398.
[14] Madison to Madison, Nov., 1786; Works, Cong. ed., vol. i, p. 253.
[15] Humphreys to Washington, Nov. 1, 1786; Sparks, Correspondence of the American Revolution, vol. iv, p. 147.

Some adventurers yet remain; they have their rendevous and their Leader. Concerning his *merits and pretensions,* even you and I my friend, have held different opinions. I know that he was a soldier of Fortune and a mercenary in Europe; and notwithstanding his affected Philanthropy and artificial Gentleness, I hold his character the same in America; the only difference is this: in Europe he received little money, and less Flattery. In America, the Sovereign of it, having added bounty to the exact Justice and possessed him of real monies exceeding in amount the life aggregate of the Revenues of a prince of the German Empire, he has, from this circumstance of preference and from the adulation of sycophants, been buoyed up to the preposterous belief, that his military Talents are superior to those of any Soldier in America. "Alieni appetens, sui profusus" was the character of the man who plotted the destruction of Rome; the same Dispositions and the like desperate Fortune mark the man who openly justifies the Conduct of the Insurgents, and who will lead them, if their cause prospers. I inclose you his performance of the 1st instant, under the signature of "Bellisarius." These opinions are his hourly conversation.[16]

General Knox transmitted to Washington a detailed analysis of the situation equally gloomy. He wrote:

On the very first impression of faction and licentiousness, the fair theoretic government of Massachusetts has given way, and its laws are trampled under foot. Men at a distance, who have admired our system of government unfounded in nature, are apt to accuse the rulers, and say that taxes have been assessed too high and collected too rigidly. This is a deception equal to any that has been hitherto entertained. That taxes may be the ostensible cause is true, but that they are the true cause is as far remote from truth as light from darkness. The people who are the insurgents have never paid any or but at most very little taxes. But they see the weakness of government: they feel at once their own poverty compared with the opulent, and their own force, and they are determined to make use of the latter to remedy the former.

Their creed is, that the property of the United States has been protected from the confiscations of Britain by the joint exertions of all, and therefore ought to be the common property of all; and he that attempts opposition to this creed is the enemy of equality and justice, and ought to be swept from the face of the earth. In a word, they are determined to annihilate all debts, public and private, and have agrarian laws, which are easily effected by the means of enforced paper money, which shall be a tender in all cases whatever. . . .

Having proceeded to this length, for which they are now ripe, we shall have a formidable rebellion against reason, the principle of all government, and against the very name of liberty.[17]

It is evident enough from these excerpts that the leaders

---

[16] King to Gerry, Nov. 5, 1786; C. R. King, Life and Correspondence of Rufus King, vol. i, p. 192. The foreign adventurer was von Steuben.

[17] Knox to Washington, Oct. 23, 1786; Noah Brooks, Henry Knox, p. 194.

of the country, rightly or wrongly, felt that they were confronted by a crisis of the first magnitude. Confiscation of property, anarchy, military dictatorship, foreign intervention seemed only just around the corner. The only remedy was to strengthen the central government.

The problem was indeed unique. Hitherto, movements in the direction of constitutional government had been motivated by the desire to establish popular rights and liberties. But, in the words of Monroe, a moderate opponent of ratification, in the Virginia convention:

> The American states exhibit at present a new and interesting spectacle in the eyes of mankind. Modern Europe, for more than twelve centuries past has presented to view one of a very different kind. In all the nations of that quarter of the globe, there hath been a constant effort on the part of the people, to extricate themselves from the oppression of their rulers; but with us the object is of a very different nature—to establish the domination of law over licentiousness—to increase the powers of the national government to such an extent, and organize it in such a manner, as to enable it to discharge its duties, and manage the affairs of state, to the best advantage.[18]

It is scarcely surprising that this class, which thus felt the very foundations of the social order threatened, should, as a part of the general swing towards authority, have experienced also a reaction unfavorable to the democratic principle. Even Washington himself declared in a private letter that the events in Massachusetts "exhibit a melancholy verification of what our transatlantic foes have predicted; and of another thing perhaps still more to be regretted—that mankind when left to themselves are unfit for their own government," [19] a state of opinion which was to find ample means of expression on the floor of the Convention.[20]

In fact, the reaction proceeded to such extremes as to engender real fears on the part of those who were attached to the principles of free government that, if they did not speedily find a remedy, even worse things might ensue.

---

[18] Elliot, Debates in the Several State Conventions, vol. iii, p. 208.
[19] Marshall, vol. v, p. 118.
[20] See, for example, the remarks of Gerry, Madison, Hamilton, Mason and Randolph on the matter, Farrand, Records of the Federal Convention, vol. i, pp. 48, 49, 51, 154, 288, 422.

The following is the matured estimate of the cautious and accurate Madison:

> It was found . . . that those least partial to popular government, or most distrustful of its efficacy, were yielding to anticipations that from an increase of the confusion a Government might result more congenial with their tastes or their opinions. Whilst those most devoted to the principles and forms of Republics, were alarmed for the cause of liberty itself, at stake in the American Experiment, and anxious for a system that would avoid the inefficacy of a mere confederacy without passing into the opposite extreme of a consolidated government. It was known that there were individuals who betrayed a bias towards Monarchy and there had always been some not unfavorable to a partition of the Union into several Confederacies.[21]

"Shall we have a King?" John Jay could ask Washington in all seriousness.[22]   And likewise he could warn him:

> What I most fear is, that the better kind of people (by which I mean the people who are orderly and industrious, who are content with their situations, and not uneasy with their circumstances) will be led by the insecurity of property, the loss of confidence in their rulers, and the want of public faith and rectitude, to consider the charms of liberty as imaginary and delusive. A taste of uncertainty and fluctuation must disgust and alarm such men, and prepare their minds for almost any change that will promise them quiet and security.[23]

The Constitution of the United States was, indeed, the honest attempt of the conservative elements of the nation to secure a framework of government that would guarantee the property rights of a minority, secure essential governmental strength and energy, and at the same time retain the fundamental ideals of a free government, as they understood the term. Their philosophy was neither that of 1776 nor that of 1922. To think of it as such, is to commit a fundamental error. To take the Constitution from its historical setting is to fail to comprehend its meaning or that of its separate parts. That faith in democracy should have grown stronger with the passing of years whose chief fruits have been to demonstrate the ability of the popular will to guide safely

---

[21] Madison, Writings (Hunt ed.), vol. i, p. 406.

[22] Jay to Washington, Jan. 7, 1787; Sparks, Correspondence, vol. iv, p. 153.

[23] Jay to Washington, June 27, 1786; Sparks, Correspondence, vol. iv, p. 134.

the course of the peoples of the world is but natural. And it will be the everlasting glory of the Fathers that they kept in mind the necessity of safeguarding the rights of the masses. Doubtless Alexander Hamilton was of all the delegates the one who was willing to go farthest in removing government from popular control. But even he, in the midst of his most vigorous inveighing against the "democratic dogma," declared:

In every community where industry is encouraged, there will be a division of it into the few and the many. Hence separate interests will arise. There will be debtors and creditors etc. Give all power to the many, they will oppress the few. Give all power to the few, they will oppress the many. Both therefore ought to have power, that each may defend itself against the other.[24]

The true philosophic basis of the second revolution of the United States which produced its present Constitution may be read in the following letter from James Madison, undoubtedly the leading philosophic student of governmental problems of the day, to Thomas Jefferson. Not only are the contents of the letter significant, but the very fact that Madison should have realized so plainly the necessity of urging on Jefferson the fundamental difference between the problems of the United States and those of France warns in unmistakable terms of the necessity under which the modern student of the Constitution finds himself of also noting the difference and its significance. In the letter he says:

Wherever the real power in a government lies, there is the danger of oppression. In our Governments the real power lies in a majority of the community, and the invasion of private rights is *chiefly* to be apprehended, not from acts of Government contrary to the sense of its constituents, but from acts in which the Government is the mere instrument of the major number of the Constituents. This is a truth of great importance, but not yet sufficiently attended to, and is probably more strongly impressed on my mind by facts and reflections suggested by them than on yours, which has contemplated abuses of power issuing from a very different quarter. Wherever there is an interest and a power to do wrong, wrong will generally be done, and not less readily by a powerful and interested party than by a powerful and interested prince. The difference, so far as it relates to the superiority of republics over monarchies, lies in the less degree of probability that interest may prompt abuses of power in the former than in the latter; and in the security in the former against an oppres-

---

[24] Farrand, Records, vol. i, p. 288.

sion of more than a smaller part of the Society, whereas, in the latter, it may be extended in a manner to the whole. . . .

It has been remarked that there is a tendency in *all* Governments to an augmentation of power at the expence of liberty. But the remark, as usually understood, does not appear to me to be well founded. Power, when it has attained a certain degree of energy and independence, goes on generally to further degrees. But when below that degree, the direct tendency is to further degrees of relaxation, until the abuses of liberty beget a sudden transition to an undue degree of power. With this explanation the remark may be true; and in the latter sense only is it, in my opinion, applicable to the existing Governments in America. It is a melancholy reflection that liberty should be equally exposed to danger whether the Government have too much or too little power.[25]

---

[25] Madison to Jefferson, Oct. 10, 1788; Works, Cong. ed., vol. i, p. 425.

CHAPTER II

STATE EXECUTIVE POWER, 1776–1787

This relation of the general trend of political thought towards strong government to the problem of executive power could almost be left to inference. As men's thoughts turned towards the establishment and maintenance of public order and ceased to focus on individual liberty, it was inevitable that the executive department of government should be the chief beneficiary of the change of emphasis. Identification by the popular mind of executive strength with the limitation of individual rights has been a common phenomenon.[1] On the other hand, the close relation of vigorous executive action to the maintenance of the orderly processes of government, and also of vested interests and the *status quo,* was too obvious to have lacked recognition by the legal-minded political leaders of the United States.

But the development of this changed attitude towards executive power is too full of interest to be summarily passed over when it is possible to trace it with accuracy, and disclose more fully its meaning and scope both in the field of state and that of national governmental experience. The purpose of the present and of the succeeding chapter is consequently to attempt to develop the more strictly governmental aspects of the general tendencies already observed, so far as they concerned executive power; to show, in fact, how the American concept of republican executive power came into being as an integral part of this phase of the evolution of American political thought.

---

[1] It is true that this is due to the fact that constitutional government has, as an all but invariable rule, come into being as a result of wresting power from an irresponsible executive, while the American Revolution was directed against parliamentary usurpation. This fact is not unimportant, but none the less, it was George III against whom the Declaration launched its thunders.

And, it must be noted, something more than a mere enumeration of the powers of state governors and of national
administrative organs is intended. The fundamental purpose will be rather to trace the evolution of the ideas which
the conservative class ultimately attained concerning the part
which the executive department ought to play in governmental life, and also to ascertain the principles of executive
organization which in 1787 were regarded as necessary for it
successfully to take this part. This point is worthy of some
insistence. To consider a department of government, in this
case the executive, as a mere arithmetic sum of individual
powers, without taking into account the fact that it is an
integral part of an organic whole, is to fail correctly to
visualize the problem. [In a study of the present sort, we
must go behind the bare words of constitutions and seek the
actual relationship of the executive officers, state and national, to other governmental organs, the part they played in
political life, their successes and failures.] A mere cata-
loguing of powers is not enough. We can attempt to discover the lessons which governmental philosophy gleaned
from contemporary experience only when we understand
what that experience really was.

If the triumph of the natural rights, individual liberty
philosophy, in which the Revolutionary movement found its
theoretic justification, operated strongly to reduce executive
prestige, practical considerations of long standing had contributed strongly to the same end. Much of colonial history
had been a repetition in little of the struggle for self-government in Great Britain, a struggle to whose traditions the
American Whigs were coheirs with their British fellows.[2]

The responsibility of the royal governor to the home government had placed him in much the same relation to the
local assemblies as that in which the Stuart kings had been

---

[2] So Jefferson wrote: " Before the Revolution we were all good English Whigs, cordial in their free principles, and in their jealousies of
their executive Magistrates. These jealousies are very apparent in
all our state constitutions " (Jefferson, Writings, Ford ed., vol. i,
p. 112).

to the Commons. It had therefore seemed necessary to the colonists to utilize every agency, and especially the control over the purse strings, to force concessions from the executive branch. The aim was always to control those powers of the government which, by virtue of the royal instructions, were in the hands of the executive, in exactly the spirit that British Parliaments had shown. In these struggles the popular assemblies were the bulwark of popular liberties, the executive departments the instrumentalities of British control. This attitude of mind could not fail profoundly to affect the original American concept of republican executive power.[3]

Relieved of all external constraint, the makers of the first American constitutions were free to translate these predilections into positive enactments. There was no longer need to concoct methods of controlling the executive. Powers could be bodily transferred to the legislature. The executive could be organized in such a fashion as to ensure complete subordination. And such, in general, was the process followed. In the words of James Wilson, "the executive and the judicial as well as the legislative authority was now the child of the people; but, to the two former, the people behaved like stepmothers. The legislature was still discriminated by excessive partiality; and into its lap, every good and precious gift was profusely thrown."[4]

An analysis of the state constitutions formed during the

---

[3] Cf. James Wilson, Works, vol. i, pp. 356–358. Wilson observes: "Before [the Revolution], the executive and the judicial powers of government were placed neither in the people, nor in those, who professed to receive them under the authority of the people. They were derived from a different and a foreign source: they were regulated by foreign maxims: they were directed to a foreign purpose. Need we be surprised, that they were objects of aversion and distrust? Need we be surprised, that every occasion was seized for lessening their influence, and weakening their energy? On the other hand, our assemblies were chosen by ourselves: they were the guardians of our rights, the objects of our confidence, and the anchor of our political hopes. Every power, which could be placed in them, was thought to be safely placed: every extension of that power was considered as an extension of our own security."

[4] Wilson, Works, vol. i, p. 357.

Revolution, and especially those constructed in the years 1776–1778,[5] affords abundant confirmation of the truthfulness of Wilson's statement. With one exception, that of New York, they included almost every conceivable provision for reducing the executive to a position of complete subordination.

Short terms, strict limitations on reëligibility, and election by the legislature[6] were the outstanding characteristics of the chief magistracy. Nor was the principle of executive unity adopted, for in the exercise of his power the chief executive was controlled by the necessity of acting in accord with the advice of an executive council chosen, save in Pennsylvania, by the legislature. The exact degree of conciliar control varied, but the general result was the same.[7] The

---

[5] The constitutions considered in this analysis are those of New Jersey, Virginia, Pennsylvania, Delaware, South Carolina (2), North Carolina and Georgia. The texts are those of Thorpe, Federal and State Constitutions. The New Jersey instrument is so incomplete as not to warrant much attention.

[6] The term of office was one year, save in South Carolina, where it was two, and Delaware, where it was three. New Jersey alone placed no restrictions on reëligibility. In Georgia the chief magistrate could hold office only a single year in three. In Georgia the choice was by the lower house alone, while in Pennsylvania choice was by joint ballot of the Council, chosen by the people, and the unicameral assembly. The provisions concerning the organization of the respective chief magistracies are Del., art. 7; Ga., arts. 2 and 13; Md., arts. 25 and 31; N. C., art. 15; S. C. (1776), arts. 3 and 13, (1775), arts. 3 and 6; N. J., arts. 1, 7 and 8; Pa., secs. 3, 19 and 22.

[7] The provisions concerning the councils are: Del., art. 8; Ga., art. 2; Md., art. 26; N. C., art. 14; S. C. (1776), arts. 5 and 13, (1778), arts. 3, 5, and 9; N. J., arts. 7 and 8; Pa., secs. 3, 19 and 22. In all these constitutions most of the enumerated executive functions were expressly subjected to control by the council. The first South Carolina constitution provided that the council's advice need be asked only where the constitution expressly required it, but in the second the matter was left entirely to legislative determination. The latter method was adopted in Maryland, where also it was provided that the council should constitute a board "for the transacting of business," in which the governor had only a single vote. The Delaware constitution provided that the governor might convene the council when he deemed it advisable, a provision made applicable in New Jersey to the whole upper chamber, which was intended, it would seem, to have special advisory functions as a whole, any three members constituting, in addition, a special council for general executive business. Both these documents are very vague, however. In North Carolina the council was "to advise the governor in the exercise of his office," a

chief magistrate was, as Governor Randolph denominated himself, only "a member of the executive."[8]

An even more fundamental weakness was the common practice of expressly submitting the exercise of either certain enumerated powers, the field of enumerated powers, or even the whole of the executive power to the legislative will. There was no opportunity for a real claim to executive independence to be made when the executive held his powers under the terms, for example, of the Virginia constitution, which declared:

> He shall, with the advice of a Council of State, exercise the executive powers of government, according to the laws of this Commonwealth; and shall not, under any pretence, exercise any power or prerogative, by virtue of any law, statute or custom of England.[9]

Language like this fairly invited legislative interference, for it was possible for the legislatures to claim, with a show of reason, that the Constitution intended that all matters concerning the executive were subject to legislative determination.

The spirit of these state conventions was precisely that of

---

similar provision being included in the Georgia instrument. These would seem blanket provisions covering all executive power. The Virginia constitution expressly subjected the executive to the necessity of conciliar advice in the exercise of all his functions. Complete subordination of the council was secured by the provision that two members should be retired by the legislature at the end of each year. In Pennsylvania all executive powers were vested in the President and Council.

[8] Edmund Randolph to Washington, Nov. 24, 1786, M. C. Conway, Omitted Chapters of History, p. 60.

[9] In this group of constitutions there is a great indefiniteness in the definitions of executive power. In New Jersey, none was attempted. In general, certain powers are specifically assigned, to be exercised for the most part with the advice of the council. Specific provision was made in some cases that some even of these enumerated powers should be exercised only subject to the law. Such was the case with the pardon power in Maryland, Delaware and North Carolina, and the power to direct the militia in Maryland. The unenumerated executive power was vested as follows: Maryland, in the governor alone, but subject to the laws, and with the Virginia prohibition against prerogative powers: North Carolina, subject to the laws. In Georgia and North Carolina all executive power was vested subject to the laws. The South Carolina instrument made no mention of unenumerated powers, nor did that of Pennsylvania. In neither, however, was there a general grant of executive power.

the French National Assembly, and their concept of executive power was well expressed by the latter body's spokesman, Tom Paine, who declared:

> With respect to what, in Europe, is called the executive . . . it is either a political superfluity or a chaos of unknown things. . . . [The executive] can be considered in [no] other light than as inferior to the legislative. The sovereign authority in any country is the power of making laws, and everything else is an official department.[10]

It was in complete accordance with this spirit that the new constitutions functioned, the legislatures refusing even to keep within the liberal constitutional limits set them, which were, in Madison's phrase, "readily overleaped by the legislature on the spur of an occasion."[11]

Jefferson described conditions in Virginia in the following language:

> All the powers of government, legislative executive and judiciary, result to the legislative body. . . . The convention, which passed the ordinance of government, laid its foundations on this basis, that the legislative, executive and judiciary departments should be separate and distinct, so that no person should exercise the powers of more than one of them at the same time. But no barrier was provided between these several powers. The judiciary and executive members were left dependent on the legislative for their subsistence in office, and some of them for their continuance in it. If therefore the legislature assumes executive and judiciary powers, no opposition is likely to be made; nor, if made, can it be effectual; because in that case they may put their proceedings in the form of an act of assembly, which will render them obligatory on the other branches. They have accordingly in many instances, decided rights which should have been left to the judiciary controversy: and the direction of the executive, during the whole time of their session, is becoming habitual and familiar.[12]

To the same effect, and without contradiction, Edmund Randolph declared in the Virginia ratification convention:

> The history of the violations of the constitution extends from the

---

[10] Paine, Rights of Man (Everyman ed.), p. 207.

[11] Madison, Writings (Hunt ed.), vol. ii, p. 40.

[12] Jefferson, Notes on Virginia; Writings (Ford ed.), vol. iii, p. 225. Jefferson furnished a detailed statement of legislative violations of the constitution to M. de Meunier in 1786. Among others were the appointment of members of the executive council as special trial judges for designated cases and the settlement of a case then pending in the courts by a legislative enactment. He adds: "The assembly is in the habitual exercise during their sessions of directing the Executive what to do. There are few pages of their journals which do not show proofs of this" (Writings, Ford ed., vol. iv, pp. 157–158).

year 1776 to the present time—violations made by formal acts of the legislature: everything has been drawn within the legislative vortex.[13]

To be sure, Jefferson contended that the Virginia situation was a special case, due to the fact that the Virginia convention had no special mandate from the people to form a government and that consequently the constitution was on the same footing as any other legislative enactment.[14] But this view was by no means generally admitted in Virginia, and certainly was not the true explanation.

Thus Richard Spaight writing of the condition of affairs in North Carolina, where there was no question of the convention's mandate, even though strongly reprobating the doctrine of judicial control, admitted that "it cannot be denied that the Assembly have passed laws unjust in themselves, and militating in their principles against the Constitution in more instances than one," and also that "it must be acknowledged that our Constitution, unfortunately, has not been proved a sufficient check to prevent the intemperate and unjust proceedings of our legislature."[15]

The significance of this legislative disregard of the constitution with respect to the position of the executive department is splendidly illustrated by the protests of the Pennsylvania council against legislative interference, a protest the more interesting as the council was chosen by the people and was vested with its powers in unequivocal language. One protest sets forth:

We should be wanting in duty to ourselves, as well as regard to the interests of the State, if we did not express our concern at the inter-

[13] Elliot, Debates, vol. iii, p. 66. See A. J. Beveridge, Life of John Marshall, vol. i, p. 393, note 1, for a discussion of Randolph's charge that the legislature had passed a bill of attainder.

[14] The matter was carefully considered in the Notes on Virginia, Writings (Ford ed.), vol. iii, p. 225 ff. Elsewhere he declared: "I have not heard that in the other states they have ever infringed their constitutions; & I suppose they have not done it; so the judges would consider any law as void which was contrary to the constitution" (Writings, Ford ed., vol. iv, p. 146). And yet both South Carolina's constitutions were expressly declared amendable by legislative act!

[15] Spaight to Iredell, Aug. 12, 1787, G. J. McRee, Life and Correspondence of James Iredell, vol. ii, p. 168.

ference of your Hon'ble House in matters merely of an Executive nature, and which have been already under the cognizance of this Board, and received a full determination.

The importunity of the petitioners has doubtless operated upon the indulgence of the house, but we flatter ourselves they rely upon the wisdom and spirit of Council in refusing their applications, where they appear inconsistent with plain positive law, or the rights of the Council, as declared by the Constitution.[16]

Another runs:

The Council having exercised the powers vested in them by the laws of the Commonwealth, with respect to sundry persons who have withdrawn themselves from the troubles of the country, and reside with the enemy, we observe sundry petitions on those subjects, defending, and resolutions calculated to rescind the determination of this Board. We have no desire to intercept the kindness and liberality of the House to petitioners of any character, but apprehend that the introducing special and particular laws to repeal the acts of the Executive branches of Government, without any conference with, or information from the Board, of the reason or ground of their proceedings, must necessarily lessen the weight of the Council, and disturb the harmony of Government.[17]

A third declares:

A desire to preserve the harmony so essential to the public welfare, has kept us silent under the various measures adopted by your House, which we conceive prejudicial to the State and derogatory to the Constitutional rights of this Board. But as we perceive a system to be adopted and steadily pursued, which evidently tends to annihilate the powers and usefulness of the Executive part of government, our duty to our constituents, and a due respect to the sacred obligations we have entered into, oblige us to speak with freedom, and to declare that as we will never make a voluntary surrender of our privileges, so we will not tamely and silently submit to any invasion of them. In the station assigned us in the government we do not apprehend ourselves obliged to take notice of any deviations from the Constitution which do not touch our own rights; but of these we conceive ourselves, in the first instance, the special and natural guardians, and when we can no otherwise prevent Legislative encroachments it is our duty at least to make a solemn appeal to the people, our mutual constituents, the true source and fountain from whence all our authority is derived. When the Constitution of this State placed the Legislative power in a single branch, with certain checks upon rash and hasty determination, it was never supposed that any House of Assembly would by special laws made for the purpose, assume the Executive powers, and by blending Legislative and Executive, unite what the Constitution had wisely and decisively separated; much less that such laws should pass without even a decent regard to those salutary restraints of time and publication, which were intended to provide against intemperate and indigested measures. It has been one of the greatest objections made to this Constitution, that it has

16 Pennsylvania Archives, Fourth Series, vol. iii, p. 762.
17 Ibid., p. 803.

left too little power in the Executive branch; and yet we see daily attempts to make that little less. We cannot suppose that it is intended practically to shew the people what mischief and abuse a single Legislature may do, and yet we are at a loss otherwise to account for those proceedings which are particularly the objects of this message.

The communication then proceeds to specify the acts in question which had produced this vigorous protest. In the first place the salaries of the judges had been reduced, with the effect, as the Council demonstrated, to "make them dependent upon the Assembly for their daily subsistence, and subject them to the strongest temptations of yielding to every veering gale of politics or party." "We conceive," they continue, "the independence of the Judges, both of the Executive and Legislative, as a point of the greatest importance to the good people of the State, and as their commissions are for seven years, unless convicted of misbehavior, it is clear that their support ought to be equally fixed and irrevocable during that period." Again, the Assembly had drawn money directly from the treasury by officers other than the Council, to whom the power had been given by the constitution. "The giving this power to any other persons, by a special law, is a violation of the Constitutional privileges of the Council—an unjust and unnecessary wound to their feelings, and calculated to lessen their influence and utility." Special commissioners, the message shows, had been appointed with powers to draw upon the treasury and to manage and conduct the defence of the Delaware. The fact that the constitution expressly declared that it was the right and duty of the Council to expedite the measures of the Assembly was ignored, inasmuch as the law expressly provided that "other persons [should] expedite the execution of [legislative] measures." This action, the Council declares, "plainly encroaches on the rights of the people, who have elected you for the purpose of devising measures, and us for that of executing them; and so far as we attempt to legislate or you to execute, so far we depart from the principles of the Constitution, usurp the rights of each other, and do injustice to the people." Another law removed the incumbents of the office of auctioneer without any complaints being lodged against them. "We cannot but consider it as a part of a system to increase your own power and lessen the weight of the Council in the eyes of the world." The Council's judgment was doubtless correct.[18]

In short, in actual operation, these first state constitutions produced what was tantamount to legislative omnipotence. The executive departments, constitutionally weak, proved even weaker in actual practice, since they were defenceless. The legislatures kept them under close supervision and control, interfered with them in their constitutional spheres, dictated to them what they should do by laws which they were unable to oppose. Separation of powers, whatever formal adherence was given the principle in bills of rights, meant the subordinate executive carrying out the legislative will.

We have excepted the constitution of New York from this discussion because of the very different state of things that resulted in that commonwealth. It is to be noted that the constitution was not completed immediately upon the outbreak of the war, going into effect only in the early spring of 1777. Governmental experience in neighboring States and in the national government had had an opportunity to make itself felt, an influence which could have reached New York, even though it did not affect, as it manifestly did not, the constitutions of South Carolina and Georgia, made in 1777 and 1778 respectively.[19] It is also to be noted that the dan-

---

[18] Pa. Archives, vol. iii, pp. 838–841. The failure of the council of censors to curb the legislature is discussed in L. H. Meader, " Council of Censors," in Pa. Mag. of Hist. and Biog., vol. xxii, p. 265. It justified, in the main, the executive complaints. See Federalist Papers, No. 48, for Madison's utilization of this experience as an argument for a strong national executive. Also G. Morris' statement, Farrand, Records, vol. ii, p. 299. For the general turbulence of Pennsylvania's history, and the consequent opposition to its popular constitution, and especially the plural executive and unicameral legislature, see S. G. Fisher, Pennsylvania: Colony and Commonwealth, chap. vi.

[19] For an example of this influence, see Edward Rutledge to Jay, Nov. 24, 1776, Jay, Correspondence and Public Papers, vol. i, p. 93; Jay to Livingston, March 22, 1777, vol. i, p. 122. In the former Rutledge wrote: " Vest the executive powers of government in an

gerous nature of the military situation of the State, the conservative nature of its population, and the fact that the individuals most influential in the construction of the constitution, Jay, Livingston and Gouverneur Morris, were, and remained, leading conservatives were all factors which contributed to establish a feasible assumption that the cause of executive strength would fare better here than in the other new States.[20]

An analysis of the executive provisions of the constitution confirms this assumption. An extremely important departure in this direction is found in the fact that the executive department was made to consist of a governor in whom was vested "the supreme executive power and authority of the State."[21] There was no privy council of the kind set up elsewhere in America, the sole remnants of the idea being found in the senatorial council of appointment[22] and the council of revision.[23]

It will be admitted that the addition of a senatorial council in the one case, and of a certain number of judges in the other, savors of that jealousy of the executive already observed. But it is easy to overemphasize this aspect of the matter. With the exception of the Maryland governor, the tool of the legislature and the executive council, and of the Pennsylvania council, which had proved so feeble, the power of appointment was uniformly in the possession of the legislature or the people. Nowhere, except in the temporary South Carolina government of 1776, was the veto power admitted. Nor is evidence lacking, indeed, that the admixture of the judges sprang from a different source than execu-

---

individual that they may have vigour, and let them be as simple as is consistent with the great outline of freedom." He was writing from Philadelphia, it should be noted.

[20] The most important account of the formation of the constitution is contained in C. Z. Lincoln, Constitutional History of New York, vol. i, chap. ii. It is generally agreed that Jay was the most influential individual in determining the final form of the constitution.

[21] N. Y. constitution, art. 17.

[22] Ibid., art. 23.

[23] Ibid., art. 3.

tive jealousy, namely, a proposal to allow judges a seat in the Senate.[24] At any rate, there was a very great difference between the privy council idea and that of the individual executive who should possess the whole executive power, subject to the participation of other members of the government in the exercise of two functions only. For the first time we have a real example of the single executive head.

Nor was the step taken without a purpose. The first draft of the constitution provided for an executive entirely of the same kind as those of the other States.[25] But the conservatives delayed completion of the document and mustered strength enough to eliminate the privy council entirely, while, at the same time, making important additions to the governor's powers.[26]

These powers were far more completely defined and more extensive than those in any other constitution save that of Pennsylvania. from which many of them were taken. The relevant portions of the constitution were as follows:

Art. XVIII. . . . The governor . . . shall by virture of his office, be general and commander in chief of all the militia, and admiral of the navy of this state; . . . he shall have power to convene the assembly and senate on extraordinary occasions; to prorogue them from time to time, provided such prorogations shall not exceed sixty days in the space of any one year; and, at his discretion, to grant reprieves and pardons to persons convicted of crimes, other than treason and murder, in which he may suspend the execution of the sentence, until it shall be reported to the legislature at their subsequent meeting: and they shall either pardon or direct the execution of the criminal, or grant a further reprieve.

Art. XIX. . . . It shall be the duty of the governor to inform the legislature at every session of the condition of the state so far as may concern his department; to recommend such matters to their consideration as shall appear to him to concern its good government, welfare, and prosperity; to correspond with the Continental Congress

[24] Lincoln, Constitutional History, vol. i, p. 537. Marginal note to draft constitution, providing "that the judges of the supreme court and chancellor of this State sit in the senate to advise and deliberate, but not to vote on any question." R. R. Livingston was the author of the article in its final form, and also the first chancellor. See Lincoln, vol. 1, pp. 554–555, for an account of adoption of this provision.

[25] For texts of the different drafts, see Lincoln, vol. 1, p. 501 ff.

[26] A draft was completed as early as October, 1776. McKesson to Clinton, Oct. 18, 1776, Clinton Papers, vol. 1, p. 297. See Sparks, Life of Gouverneur Morris, vol. 1, p. 120.

and other States; to transact all necessary business with the officers of government, civil and military; to take care that the laws are executed to the best of his ability; and to expedite all such measures as may be resolved upon by the legislature.

To these, of course, are to be added the important powers of qualified appointment and qualified veto. It is to be observed also that there is no question of the interposition of the law of the land to regulate these powers. They are the governor's, by direct grant of the people, and his alone.

Another distinguishing characteristic, equally important, is the fact that the governor was to be chosen by a constitutionally defined electorate, not by the legislature. He was also to have a three-year term, and there were to be no limitations on his reëligibility to office. In short, all the isolated principles of executive strength in other constitutions were here brought into a new whole. Alone they were of slight importance; gathered together they gain new meaning. And, in addition, we have new elements of strength utilized for the first time on the American continent.

The proof of the pudding is the eating, and the New York constitution stands the test. For the first eighteen years of its existence the chief magistracy was in the hands of one man, George Clinton. From the standpoint of executive vigor, it could not have been in better, for he was, as Governor Morris characterized him, a man " who had an aversion to councils, because, to use his own words, the duty of looking out for danger makes men cowards." [27]

The spirit of his long administration found prophetic expression in his first gubernatorial message to the legislative houses:

The late convention, having in their plan of government, manifested the most scrupulous attention to the freedom and happiness of the people, and by marking the line between the Executive, Legislative and Judicial powers, wisely provided for the security of each, it becomes our duty to second their endeavors; and as our conduct will in some measure be a rule for those who are hereafter entrusted with the administration of government, let us remain within the several departments in which the constitution has placed us, and thereby pre-

[27] J. L. Jenkins, Lives of the Governors of the State of New York, p. 70.

serve the same inviolate, and repay the trust reposed in us by our constituents, when they made us the guardians of their rights.

I do not urge this, gentlemen, because I conceive the caution necessary to you; but to shew you the important light in which I see this object, and to convince you (however unequal I may find myself for the task) that it shall always be my strenuous endeavor, on the one hand, to retain and exercise for the advantage of the people the powers with which they have invested me; on the other, carefully to avoid the invasions of the rights which the constitution has placed in other persons.[28]

A study of the Clinton Papers, the gubernatorial messages to the legislature[29] and the records of the council of revision[30] reveals that Clinton kept his word. From the time when he exercised his independent control over the militia to rush reinforcements to relieve the critical military situation that existed when he was sworn into office (July 30, 1777),[31] until he surrendered the reins of office, his administration was characterized by a vigorous use of the powers with which the constitution invested him. He constantly suggested matters for legislative action, and generally laws were passed in accordance with his suggestions.[32] When the evacuation of New York left the southern part of the State without government, his actions in the direction of restoring and maintaining law and order were of such a kind that even Alexander Hamilton, in a caustic campaign attack, found in them little to criticise.[33] A legislature that threatened to surrender what he regarded as New York's just claims in the Vermont region was threatened with proroguement.[34] The so-called "Doctors' Riots" in New York City were put down by the militia, and remnants of Shay's insurrectionists who fled to New York were routed out.[35] And, what was more impor-

[28] Clinton Papers, vol. ii, p. 297.
[29] State of New York, Messages of Governors (C. Z. Lincoln ed.).
[30] A. R. Street, Council of Revision of the State of New York.
[31] Clinton Papers, vol. ii, p. 122 ff.
[32] See Lincoln, Messages, passim, and especially the footnotes indicating what recommended measures were adopted.
[33] Hamilton, Works (Lodge ed.), vol. i, pp. 512–513.
[34] Benson to Jay, Nov. 7, 1781; Jay, Correspondence, vol. ii, p. 151.
[35] Jenkins, Lives of the Governors, pp. 71–72; Minot, History of the Insurrections in Massachusetts, pp. 155–156.

tant still, as a member of the council of revision, Clinton joined in vetoing no fewer than fifty-eight legislative enactments in the ten years prior to the convening of the Federal Convention alone.[36]

While thus abating no whit the ideals of executive power which he had enunciated in his first message, Clinton was able at the same time to rise to the position of dominating the political life of the whole State, and this despite the fact that he lacked the support of the most influential leaders of the State, such as Schuyler, Hamilton, Jay and Morris.[37] The vigor, as well as the lack of success, of the campaigns of 1789 and 1792 testify to the importance that the office had attained in the constitutional system and political life of the State. One need only read the campaign documents prepared against Clinton by Hamilton in 1789 to see the evident importance that the author of them attached to the office,[38] as one needs only follow the course of the anti-impost, antinational party in New York prior to 1787 to understand that it was Clinton who was its head and front.[39]

"It is seriously to be deplored," Hamilton wrote, "that dissension reigns in the most important departments of the State, and as dissensions among brethren, so destructive to the happiness of families, are often appeased by parental influence, so there is good reason to flatter ourselves that a Chief Magistrate, sincerely desirous of re-establishing concord, may without much difficulty effect it, especially if he should owe his exaltation to the votes of both contending parties."[40] One doubts whether the parental comparison could, or would, have been used in any other Commonwealth on the Continent.

In fact, by 1789 Hamilton was ready to charge that the

---

[36] Figures compiled from Street, Council of Revision.

[37] See Hamilton, Works (Lodge ed.), vol. i, pp. 521–522, 524.

[38] Ibid., pp. 514 ff., 518 ff.

[39] "Le Gouverneur de New York est l'ennemi le plus dangereux de la puissance du Congrès" (Otto to Montmorin, July 25, 1787, Farrand, Records, vol. iii, p. 61).

[40] Hamilton, Works (Lodge ed.), vol. i, p. 514.

governor had, through the control that he exercised over the council of appointment, built up a party machine that enabled him to retain his hold on the office and at the same time control, in large measure, the legislative branch. Modern researches have disproved this charge to a considerable degree,[41] and doubtless Hamilton's accounts were exaggerated for party purposes, but one can not fail to see the significance of the fact that the charges could be made with at least a show of reasonableness, nor to believe that, in a day when clamor for public office was the equal of any that has since been known, the control of the patronage could have failed to be of tremendous influence. It was to experience, at any rate, that Hamilton appealed when he wrote:

Whether an improper or excessive influence has in fact been derived from the use of that engine [the council of appointment], those who have been àttentive to the progress of public affairs must decide for themselves. Appearances must be carefully consulted, and if there are instances in which members of the Legislature have been seen to change one party or system disagreeable to the Governor, for another system agreeable to him, and if that change of conduct, has been observed to be speedily followed by the reception of lucrative appointment the conclusion from such a fact would be irresistible.[42]

As effective a weapon in maintaining the independence of the executive as the patronage was the veto power, a power which the council exercised in full accord with the spirit of the constitution. The constitutional reason assigned for its creation was because "laws inconsistent with the spirit of this constitution or with the public good may be hastily or inadvisedly passed."[43] With this constitutional justification, the council proceeded to object to laws on either ground

[41] J. M. Gitterman, "New York Council of Appointment," in Pol. Sci. Quart., vol. vii, p. 94. The author's general conclusions are that the governor's appointments were mainly non-partisan, but that his control of patronage was politically valuable. See also H. L. McBain, "DeWitt Clinton and the Origin of the Spoils System in New York," in Columbia Studies in History, Economics and Political Science, vol. xxviii, No. 1.

[42] Hamilton, Works (Lodge ed.), vol. i, p. 527. Clinton successfully maintained the disputed right to prior nomination, and so controlled appointments. For the right of prior nomination, see Lincoln, Messages, vol. ii, p. 473. For Clinton's control, see Hamilton, Works, vol. i, pp. 525–527.

[43] New York constitution, art. iii.

with complete freedom. By far the larger portion of these objections were, however, based on constitutional reasons. The result was that in New York alone, prior to 1787, there was built up a body of constitutional interpretation, in which, indeed, may be found some of the most important of American constitutional principles.[44]

The importance of this can be hardly overrated. For the first time we have in practice a legislature actually limited by the constitution. Constitutional limitations become something more than pious wishes, and constitutional provisions for separation of powers pass from the realm of governmental theory into positive law. The executive and judiciary gained in proportion as the legislature lost. The interests of both were enlisted in keeping the legislature in bounds, and there is no evidence of friction.

The practical value of the veto obtained one striking illustration. One complaint of the Pennsylvania executive council had been, as we have seen, that the legislature created special bodies to which were assigned various functions vested by the constitution in the council, and which were independent of it. This was carried out in New York on a large scale immediately after the inauguration of the new government. The recently convened legislature resolved itself into a convention and created a council of safety, of which the governor was only a member with a casting vote. In this council it vested practically unlimited and uncontrolled power and adjourned.[45]

---

[44] See, for example, Street, Council of Revision, p. 214 ff. In this message the council vetoed a tax bill, among other reasons "because an equal right to life, liberty and property is a fundamental principle in all free societies and States and is intended to be secured to the people of this State by the Constitution thereof; and, therefore, no member of this State can constitutionally or justly be constrained to contribute more to the support thereof than in like proportion with the other citizens, according to their respective estates and abilities." This example, foreshadowing as it does the Supreme Court's doctrine of the substantive concept of 'due process of law,' is an excellent illustration of the nature of the council of revision's work. The principle of judicial control evidently was here highly developed.

[45] Lincoln, Messages, vol. ii, pp. 15-17.

The new government, in an almost unorganized condition, was unable to prevent this highly unconstitutional procedure. As soon as possible, however, the governor reconvened the legislature, though not without objections from at least one member of the council,[46] and restored the regular constitutional processes.

The council of revision made vigorous attempts to prevent the recognition of the legal validity of any action of this irregular body, but the legislature overruled them. The day of the executive was yet to come. In 1780 a second attempt was made to create a council with both legislative and executive powers. The council promptly vetoed the measure, and this time were upheld.

The constitutional reasons assigned for this veto were of the utmost significance. They were:

Because to take the several measures in the bill directed to be taken, the person administering the Government, with the Council therein provided, must exercise the power of legislation; which, by the Constitution, is vested in the Senate and Assembly, and cannot by them be delegated to others. 2nd. Because the person administering the government is by the bill subjected in the exercise of his office, to the control of a Council, when by the Constitution, it is expressly ordained, determined, and declared, *that the supreme executive power and authority of this State shall be vested in a Governor.*[47]

Constitutional government in New York and constitutional government elsewhere thus meant quite different things. In the other States we find legislative supremacy, executive subordination, a non-controlling constitution. Whatever the

---

[46] John Morin Scott to Clinton, Nov. 21, 1777, Clinton Papers, vol. ii, p. 532.

[47] Lincoln, Messages, vol. ii, p. 113. The italics are in the original. Considerable light is thrown on the operation of the veto by the following excerpt from a letter to Clinton from a member of the legislature: "I esteem our form of government better than any I have yet been acquainted with. And I think the Council of Revision a good check at sometimes on the precipitate Act of Both Houses. I'll instance that of the Confiscation Bill. And I was straniously for selling, but when you gave your reason for the contrary, you fully convinc't me I was wrong, and from that time I made use of your objections for suspending the sale of the Principal Estates which had the desired affect; and I strove to convince the People as much as possible your views were for their good (Wills to Clinton, Dec. 7, 1781, Clinton Papers, vol vii, p. 560).

theory, there was legislative omnipotence of exactly the type found today in continental countries possessing written constitutions. The legislature was sovereign. In New York the council of revision made the constitution, in reality as in theory, a controlling instrument, the people's charter to government. Executive independence and executive equality with the legislature became a fact. The one man who possessed the executive powers vested in him by the constitution exercised them in accordance with his own judgment. Since he gave satisfaction to the people, he was returned to office. With the power of popular approval and the patronage at his disposal, he was able to become the dominant political force in political life, until by the period of the making of the Federal Constitution possession of the governor's chair and control of state policy had become synonymous. In short, here was a strictly indigenous and entirely distinctive constitutional system, and, of course, executive department, for the consideration of the Philadelphia delegates.

It was an easier task for this concept of executive power to take root in conservative New York than in two such typical New England commonwealths as Massachusetts and New Hampshire, especially since in both the completed constitutions were submitted for popular ratification. It is the more significant, consequently, that even there a distinctive trend towards executive strength is observable.

At the outset of the Revolution, Massachusetts had been content to revert to the governmental forms provided by its suspended charter. Since there was no longer a royal governor, executive power was placed in the hands of a council of twenty-eight.[48]

The success of this body was but slight. A contemporary observer described the situation as follows: "There is great expectation of a new form of government in our state. I hope it will be a good one, and an executive power will be

---

[48] H. A. Cushing, History of the Transition from Provincial to Commonwealth Government, pp. 176–178.

lodged somewhere; at present, if there is any, you would be puzzled to find it; hence the chariot wheels drive so slowly." [49]

These expectations were, however, grievously disappointed. The concept of a strong executive was evidently no favorite of those responsible for the document submitted by the Convention in 1778 for popular ratification.[50] Election was to be by the voters,[51] but with this exception, all of the familiar evidences of jealousy of the executive were included. The governor was to hold office for only a single year. He was to be controlled in the exercise of his functions by the upper chamber or the legislature as a whole. He was, for example, to exercise the military power "according to the laws . . . or the resolves of the General Court," [52] while the advice of the Senate was required to call extra sessions, declare embargoes, or make such appointments as were placed in executive hands.[53] When the advice of the Senate was required, the governor had only a single vote.[54] The pardon power was vested in the governor, the lieutenant-governor and the speaker.[55] There was no provision for a veto power, or any other organic control of the legislature.

But this constitution failed of ratification, and in the process of rejection the various towns drafted addresses in which were included the objections which led to their action, and also constructive recommendations of principles which they desired to see embodied in a new instrument. Easily the most important of these was the so-called "Essex Result." This document, from the pen of a future State chief justice, may be fairly considered as representative of conservative Massachusetts opinion.[56]

---

[49] Samuel Otis to Gerry, Nov. 22, 1777, J. T. Austin, Life of Elbridge Gerry, vol. I, p. 266.
[50] The text of this constitution is given in Bradford, History of Massachusetts, vol. ii, p. 349 ff.
[51] Massachusetts constitution (1778), art. v.
[52] Art. xvii.
[53] Arts. xvii and xxi.
[54] Art. xxii.
[55] Art. xxiii.
[56] The text of the Essex Result may be found in T. Parsons, Memoir of Theophilus Parsons, appendix I, p. 359 ff.

Its criticisms of the proposed executive department are illuminating.[57]   It was objected that the governor ought not to be a member of the Senate (he was its president) ; that the property qualifications of the office were too low; that the executive powers were too small; that the Senate's control over the executive was improper—in the words of the Result, "the supreme executive office is not vested with sufficient authority . . . and an independence between the executive and legislative authority is not preserved"; that the method of making appointments was exceptionable; and that the pardon power was improperly divided.[58]

The positive recommendations of the Result were moderate, but significant.   The participation of the Senate as such in the business of the executive department should be eliminated, but in its place an advisory privy council should be installed.   The governor should possess the power to appoint and remove all militia officers.   Subject to the advice of his council, he should have complete control of calling the armed forces into service and of regulating them.   The appointing power of the governor should be extended to include judges and the attorney-general.[59]   And, most important of all, the veto power should be given him.

The arguments in behalf of these changes will illustrate the influence of the experience of those States which enjoyed the doubtful blessing of uncontrolled popular assemblies. Full quotations seem justified.   Concerning the veto power, the Result argued as follows:

We now want only to give the executive power a check upon the legislative, to prevent the latter from encroaching on the former and stripping it of all its rights. The legislative in all states hath attempted it where this check was wanting, and have prevailed, and the freedom of the state was thereby destroyed. This attempt has resulted from that lust of domination, which in some degree influences all men, and all bodies of men. The Governor therefore with the consent of the privy council, may negative any law, proposed to be enacted by the legislative body. The advantages which will attend

[57] Seven of eighteen specific objections concerned the executive.
[58] Parsons, pp. 359–361.
[59] The general principles concerning executive power may be found in Parsons, pp. 379–382.

the due use of this negative are, that thereby the executive power will be preserved entire—the encroachments of the legislative will be repelled, and the powers of both properly balanced. All the business of the legislative body will be brought to one point, and subject to an impartial consideration on a regular consistent plan. As the Governor will have it in his charge to state the situation of the government to the legislative body at the opening of every session, as far as his information will qualify him, therefore, he will now know officially all that has been done, with what design the laws were enacted, how far they have answered the purposed end, and what still remains to compleat the intention of the legislative body. The reasons why he will not make an improper use of his negative are—his annual election—the annual election of the privy council, by and out of the legislative body—His political character and honor are at stake—If he makes a proper use of his negative by preserving the executive powers entire, by pointing out any mistake in the laws which may escape any body of men through inattention, he will have the smiles of the people. If on the contrary, he makes an improper use of his negative, and wantonly opposes a law that is for the public good, his reputation, and that of his privy council are forfeited, and they are disgracefully tumbled from their seats. This Governor is not appointed by a King, or his ministry, nor does he receive instructions from a party of men, who are pursuing an interest diametrically opposite to the good of the state; and he knows he must soon return and sink to a level with the rest of the community. The danger is he will be too cautious of using his negative in the interest of the state. His fear of offending may prompt him, if he is a timid man, to yield up some parts of his executive powers.[60]

The arguments for gubernatorial control of the militia and exercise of the power of appointment are equally illuminating:

Was one to propose a body of militia, over which two Generals, with equal authority, should have command, he would be laughed at. Should one pretend, that the General should have no controul over his subordinate officers, either to remove them or to supply their posts, he would be pitied for his ignorance of the subject he was discussing. It is obviously necessary, that the man who calls the militia to action, and assumes the military controul of them in the field, should precisely know the number of his men, their equipments and residence, and the talents and tempers of the several ranks of officers, and their respective departments in the State, that he may wisely determine to whom the necessary orders are to be issued. Regular and particular returns of these requisites should be frequently made. Let it be inquired, are these returns to be made only to the legislative body, or a branch of it, which necessarily moves slow?—Is the General to go to them for information? intreat them to remove an improper officer, and give him another they shall chuse? and in fine is he to supplicate his orders from them, and constantly walk where their leading-strings shall direct his steps? If so, where are the power and force of the militia—where the union—where the despatch and profound secrecy? Or shall these returns be made to him? when he may see with his own eyes—be his own judge of the

---

[60] Parsons, p. 397.

merit, or demerit of his officers—discern their various talents and qualifications, and employ them as the service and defence of his country demand. . . . It may be further observed here that if the subordinate civil or military executive officers are appointed by the legislative body or a branch of it, the former will become dependent upon the latter, and the necessary independence of either the legislative or executive powers upon the other is wanting. The legislative power will have that undue influence over the executive which will amount to a controul, for the latter will be their creatures, and will fear their creators.[61]

Such is the temper of mankind, that each man will be liable to introduce his own friends and connexions into office, without regarding the public interest. If one man or a small number appoint, their connexions will probably be introduced. If a large number appoint, all their connexions will receive the same favour. The smaller the number appointing, the more contracted their connexions, and for that reason, there will be a greater probability of better officers, as the connexions of one man or a very small number can fill but a very few of the offices. When a small number of men have the appointment, or the management in any particular department, their conduct is accurately noticed. On any miscarriage or imprudence the public resentment lies with weight. All the eyes of the people are converted to a point, and produce that attention to their censure, and the fear of misbehavior which are the greatest security the state can have, of the wisdom and prudence of its servants. This observation will strike us when we recollect that many a man will zealously promote an affair in a public assembly, of which he is but one of a large number, yet, at the same time, he would blush to be thought the sole author of it. For all these reasons, the supreme executive power should be rested in the hands of a small number, who should have the appointment of all subordinate executive officers.[62]

The constitution finally adopted in 1780 embodied many of the conservative ideas of the New York constitution in respect to executive strength. Annual choice by the voters,[63] a privy council " for advising the governor in the executive part of the government," and for "ordering and directing the affairs of the commonwealth, according to the laws of the land," [64] the possession by the governor of the military powers, subject to the law,[65] of the pardon power,[66] a considerable portion of the civil appointing power,[67] and, most

[61] Ibid., p. 380.
[62] Ibid., p. 381.
[63] Chap ii, sec. i, arts i, ii, and iii.
[64] Chap. ii, sec. iii, arts. i and iv.
[65] Chap. ii, sec. i, art. vii.
[66] Chap. ii, sec. i, art. viii.
[67] Chap. ii, sec. i, arts. viii and ix. But military officers were to be elected either by the troops or by electoral colleges of officers.

important of all, the qualified veto power,[68]—these were the chief features of the new executive. It was evidently a compromise product of conservative wishes and popular prejudices.

The same rise in prestige in the executive department in conservative circles which is apparent in Massachusetts is revealed by the constitutional history of New Hampshire, and also the same enduring popular jealousy of the chief magistrate. In January, 1776, temporary governmental arrangements—there was nothing that deserves the name constitution—were made, which included no formal provision for an executive department at all, the omission being supplied by an extra-constitutional council of safety.[69] As in Massachusetts, this worked badly. The expense of so large a body and " the delay necessarily occasioned by the business of the executive department being intrusted to so great a number of persons, have been too sensibly felt to require arguments on our part, to convince you that an alteration in this respect will promote the interest of every individual in the community," declared one of the addresses that accompanied a proposed constitution.[70]

Exactly the same note was struck by these addresses as in the Essex Result. The growing importance of a well-constructed executive department is eloquently evidenced, for example, in the following excerpt, in which it was declared to the voters:

This power is the active principle of all governments : it is the soul, and without it the body politic is but a dead corpse. Its department is to put in execution all the laws enacted by the legislative body. It ought, therefore, to have the appointment of all the civil officers of the State. It is at the head of the militia, and therefore should have equally the appointment of all the military officers within the same. Its characteristic requisites are secrecy, vigour, and despatch. The fewer persons, therefore, this supreme power is trusted with, the greater probability there is that these requisites will be found. The

---

[68] Chap. i, sec. i, art. ii.
[69] Town Papers, Documents and Records Relating to Towns in New Hampshire, vol. ix, p. 846. For text see Documents and Records Relating to the State of New Hampshire, vol. viii, pp. 2–4.
[70] Town Papers, vol. ix, 849.

convention, therefore, on the maturest deliberation, have thought it best to lodge this power in the hands of one, whom they have stiled the GOVERNOR. They have, indeed, array'd him with honours, they have armed him with power, and set him on high. But still he is only the right hand of *your* power, and the mirror of *your* majesty. Every possible provision is made to guard against the abuse of this high betrustment and protect the rights of the people. He can take no one step of importance without the advice of his privy-council; and he is elected annually. But as this was too little, no one person is capable of being elected oftener than three years in seven. Every necessary and useful qualification is required in him, in point of age, religion, residency, and fortune. In addition to all which, he is liable for every misconduct to be impeached, tried, and displaced, by the two legislative branches; and is amenable to the laws besides, equally with the meanest subject of the State. Thus controlled and checked against himself the Convention thought it reasonable and necessary, that he, in turn, should have the right of objecting to and suspending, tho' not the absolute control over the acts of that body; which they thought indispensably necessary to repel any encroachments on the executive power, and preserve its independency.[71]

Democratic forces in New Hampshire were too strong to permit either the adoption of the veto clause or even the retention of so hated a title as that of Governor. For the rest, ultimately the provisions of the Massachusetts constitution were adopted. But in conservative circles new language was being spoken concerning the importance of the executive, the desirability of one-man rule, and the rôle of this individual executive in state life.

The experiences with the state governments during the period following the cessation of hostilities served further to confirm these tendencies towards increasing confidence in the executive and increasing distrust of the legislature. A review of those practical factors enumerated in the preceding chapter as the active causes of the convening of the Philadelphia convention reveals the state legislatures as the main instruments of evil. It was these bodies which had originated and multiplied most of the difficulties which the Constitution was intended to remedy. From them came the paper money and debtor laws. It was also they who adopted the retaliatory commercial restrictions which played havoc with commercial prosperity. Especially was it true that the lower house proved the stronghold of the popular party.

---

[71] Ibid., vol. ix, p. 849.

The experience of Massachusetts during the insurrection is a case in point. Governor Bowdoin acquitted himself well, from the standpoint of the conservatives. His executive measures were vigorous, albeit moderate. The senate supported the action of the executive wholeheartedly, but the house of representatives proved a haven of refuge for the discontented. To this effect writes the contemporary historian of the insurrection:

> While the Supreme Executive was employed in making the necessary military arrangements, for supporting the administration of justice, the House of Representatives remained in the same pacifick disposition towards the insurgents. Nothing of consequence was suffered to pass them, but what was connected with the grievances of the people. . . . Such delays taking place in the effecting of a vigorous system for the authority of the laws, occasioned very great alarms among those who were most opposed to the insurrections. . . . They began to lose confidence in the General Court, and to wish that means might be found to adjourn them, before the publick cause should be injured by a feeble system, which might tend to hold up their divisions and want of energy.
>
> There also began to arise another class of men in the community, who gave very serious apprehensions to the advocates of a republican form of government These, though few in number, and but the seeds of a party, consisted of persons respectable for their literature and their wealth. They . . . were almost ready to assent to a revolution, in hopes of erecting a political system, more braced than the present, and better calculated, in their opinions, to promote the peace and happiness of the citizens.[72]

Indeed, the injustice, mutability and multiplicity of state laws brought home to the conservatives even the truth, which Mill was subsequently to elucidate, that legislative bodies are incompetent legislators. In his thoughtful analysis of the causes of the second revolution, Madison wrote:

> As far as the laws are necessary to mark with precision the duties of those who obey them and to take from those who are to administer them a discretion which might be abused, their number is the price of liberty. As far as they exceed this limit, they are a nuisance, a nuisance of the most persistent kind. Try the Codes of the several States by this test, and what a luxuriancy of legislation do they present. The short period of independency has filled as many pages as the century which preceded it. Every year almost every session adds a new volume. . . .
> We daily see laws repealed or superseded, before any trial can

---

[72] Minot, Insurrections, pp. 120–163 and passim. The value of the veto was proved by Bowdoin's successful opposition to a measure reducing the governor's salary (Minot, Insurrections, pp. 166–169).

have been made their merits, and even before a knowledge of them can have reached the remoter districts within which they are to operate.[73]

The spoliation of the "College" in Pennsylvania and the bitter attack on the Bank of North America indicated only too well the animus of many of these laws, namely, the destruction of vested interests. The following tax law of New York, of whose purpose we may approve, points in the same direction, and shows even more plainly the validity of the complaints against the legislature:

Whereas, many persons in this State, *taking advantage* of the necessities of this country, *have*, in prosecuting their private gain, amassed *large sums* of money to the great prejudice of the public, and ought therefore to pay an extraordinary tax, and it will be impossible for the assessors, with any degree of certainty, to ascertain the profits made by such persons in manner aforesaid, be it therefore enacted . . . that the assessors shall . . . assess *all such persons* . . . at such rates . . . as they, the assessors shall . . . think proper.[74]

John Marshall could well say, with customary lucidity:

In the state governments generally no principle had been introduced which could resist the wild projects of the moment, give the people an opportunity to reflect, and allow the good sense of the nation time for exertion. The uncertainty with respect to measures of great importance to every member of the community, the instability of principles which ought if possible to be rendered immutable produced a long train of ills. . . . The direct consequence was the loss of confidence in the government and in individuals.[75]

Executive strength was such a principle. This was, in fact, the chief teaching of state experience. It could not have been otherwise, for the cause of executive power and executive independence had been too often identified with the cause of representative government as opposed to the rule of popular committees, with the cause of orderly governmental processes as opposed to legislative disregard of constitutional principles, with, and this was vital, the whole cause of property and established rights, for that department not to rise in the scale of conservative esteem. In short, the

---

[73] Madison, Writings (Hunt ed.), vol. v, pp. 365–366. Cf. Jefferson to Madison, Dec. 20, 1787; Jefferson, Writings (Ford ed.), vol. iv, p. 480.
[74] Street, Council of Revision, p. 214.
[75] Marshall, Washington, vol. v, p. 87.

change of emphasis from liberty to authority had meant a corresponding change of emphasis from the legislature to the executive.

State experience thus contributed, nothing more strongly, to discredit the whole idea of the sovereign legislature, to bring home the real meaning of limited government and co-ordinate powers. The idea, more than once utilized as the basis of the explanation of Article II of the Constitution, that the jealousy of kingship was a controlling force in the Federal Convention, is far, very far, from the truth. The majority of the delegates brought with them no far-reaching distrust of executive power, but rather a sobering conscious-ness that, if their new plan should succeed, it was necessary for them to put forth their best efforts to secure a strong, albeit safe, national executive.

Madison but expressed the general conservative view when he declared on the Convention floor:

Experience had proved a tendency in our governments to throw all power into the legislative vortex. The Executives of the States are in general little more than cyphers; the legislatures omnipotent. If no effective check be devised for restraining the instability and en-croachment of the latter, a revolution of some kind or the other would be inevitable. The preservation of Republican Government therefore required some expedient for the purpose, but required evidently that in devising it the genuine principles of that form should be kept in view.[76]

With the exception of the New York executive and, with reservations, that of Massachusetts, the state executive was, it is evident, in no sense of the word a model to be followed in the creation of the national executive. A meticulous cal-culation of the proportion of state constitutions granting this or that presidential power to their chief magistrate does not at all affect the truth of this statement. The conservatives desired something besides a mere cypher for a national exec-utive.

And yet state experience had a definite, positive value. It taught that executive energy and responsibility are in-

[76] Farrand, Records, vol. ii, p. 35. Cf. Federalist Papers, No. 48, for a fuller development of this idea.

versely proportional to executive size; that, consequently, the
one-man executive is best. It taught the value of integration; the necessity of executive appointments, civil and military; the futility of legislative military control. It demonstrated the necessity for the veto as a protective measure.
It showed that this power could be utilized as a means of
preventing unwise legislation. It even, if we accept the
argument of the Essex Result,[77] revealed the desirability of
bringing legislative business into a single whole by the executive department. It demonstrated the value of a fixed executive salary which the legislature could not reduce. It discredited choice by the legislature, though without teaching
clearly the lesson of popular choice, for, after all, the people
chose a Clinton instead of a Schuyler and replaced a Bowdoin by a Hancock. And, above all, it assured the acceptance of, if it did not create, a new concept of constitutional
government—the fundamental principles of which were the
ruling constitution, the limited legislature, and the three
equal and coördinate departments.

There is no need to point out that the New York governorship in large measure fulfilled the requirements of the concept thus attained. The relatively fixed constitutional principles of that State, a result chiefly of the Council of
Revision's action, and of its vigorous, dominating executive,
known only too well to the leaders of the national party,

---

[77] " All the business of the legislative body will be brought to one
point, and subject to an impartial consideration on a regular consistent plan. As the Governor will have it in charge to state the
situation of the government to the legislative body at the opening of
every session, as far as his information will qualify him therefor,
he will know officially all that has been done, what design the laws
were enacted, how far they have answered the purposed end, and what
still remains to compleat the intention of the legisative body " (Parsons, Memoir, p. 397). Cf. Madison's suggestion that " a standing
committee composed of a few select and skilful individuals should
be appointed to prepare bills on all subjects which they may judge
proper to be submitted to the Legislature at their meetings," its members to hold no other office (Madison to Caleb Wallace, Aug. 23,
1785; Writings, Hunt ed., vol. ii, pp. 168–169). The Pennsylvania
executive council actually presented the heads of a bill for legislative
determination, although with dubious success. (See W. B. Reed,
Life and Correspondence of Joseph Reed, vol. ii, pp. 173–178.)

caused it quite generally to be accepted as the best of the state governments. Here, and here only, was a satisfactory model.

It was in significant language that John Jay, from the midst of the turbulence of Pennsylvania's political life, expressed to the chief executive of his State this approval:

The exceeding high opinion entertained here of your Constitution and the wisdom of your Counsels, has made a deep impression on many People of wealth and Consequence in this State, who are dissatisfied with their own; and unless their opinions should previously be changed, will remove to New York the moment the Enemy leave it. Mr. Gerard (who seems better acquainted with Republics than almost any man I have ever known) has passed many Enconiums on our Constitution & Government, and I am persuaded no Circumstance will conduce more to the Population of our Country by migrations from others, than the Preservation of its vigor and Reputation.

This unhappy city is all Confusion; the Government wants nerves, and the public Peace has for some Days been destroyed by mobs and Riots which seem to defy the authority of the magistrate. This is one of the Fruits of their whimsical Constitution, and of the Countenance given to Committees & let Politicians learn from this, to dread the least Deviation from the Line of Constitutional authority. *Obsta principiis,* is a good maxim, but all have not sufficient Decision in their conduct to observe it. Government once relaxed is not easily braced. And it is far more difficult to reassume Powers than permit them to be taken and executed by those who have no right by the Constitution to hold them.[78]

---

[78] Jay to Clinton, Oct. 7, 1779, Clinton Papers, vol. v, p. 311. Cf. Duer to Jay, May 28, 1777, Jay, Correspondence, vol. i, p. 137; Jay to Gansevoort, June 5, 1777, Jay Correspondence, vol. i, p. 140; Adams, Works, vol. iii, p. 59; Hamilton to Morris, May 7, 1777, Works (Lodge ed.), vol. vii, p. 493; May 19, 1777, p. 497.

CHAPTER III

NATIONAL EXECUTIVE POWER, 1776–1787

It is manifestly not within the scope of the present study to undertake a complete investigation of the solution given the problem of national executive power prior to 1787. To do so would be to duplicate work that has in large measure been satisfactorily done,[1] and would, in any event, transcend the limits both of time and space available for a doctoral dissertation. Our purpose will be rather, as in the preceding chapter, to go behind the details and search for the tendencies of governmental thought produced by national experience and for the principles of executive organization which this experience seemed to dictate.

For the sake of clarity, however, it may be well to restate the problem with which the revolutionists were confronted. The general scope of national power was determined on the one hand by the mere fact of war, on the other by the peculiar domestic situation. Thus the national governing body was obliged, since it was at war, to create an army and a navy, to recruit them, officer them, arm them, supply them, and determine their use and movements. To do these things, money was necessary, and so a revenue had to be raised and expended, accounts kept and an audit system created. When

---

[1] The most important work on the general field is H. B. Learned, President's Cabinet. Chapters ii to v cover the period of the formation of the Constitution. The writer desires to make especial acknowledgment of his indebtedness to Professor Learned's bibliography. An older, but valuable, study is " The Development of the Executive Departments, 1775–1789 " in Essays in the Constitutional History of the United States in the Formative Period, J. F. Jameson, ed. C. O. Paulin, Navy of the American Revolution, contains a complete and scholarly account of the development of the Marine Department during the Revolution. L. C. Hatch, Administration of the American Army, is inadequate. Francis Wharton's discussion of the two schools of political leaders, the " liberative " and the " constructive," is, of course, a classic. F. Wharton, Revolutionary Diplomatic Correspondence of the United States, vol. i, chap. i.

independence came to be the aim of the revolutionists, there arose the additional necessity of establishing and maintaining relations with such members of the family of nations as would enter into them.

The composition and organization of the national governing body was as plainly determined by the fact that the revolutionary movement involved thirteen governmental units lacking any prior formal organic connection the one with the other. Representatives of these units, coming together in the first instance for purposes of discussion, were forced by the pressure of events to undertake the business of government. But the corporate body did not lose for that reason its essential character of a council of ambassadors. Consequently votes were taken by States, and, after formal ratification of the Articles, a high proportion of affirmative votes was required for any important positive action.

Strict limitations on the power of this Congress also resulted from the domestic situation. In fact, Congress was prevented by it from becoming a legislative body at all. It could work out general policies, but could not enforce them, except over against the officers of its own creation. It was totally without power to lay down general rules of conduct to which all citizens should conform, subject to penalty. Despite its name, the counterpart of Congress in the state organization was the state council of the Maryland type.[2] Its activities from first to last were necessarily executive, in the modern sense of the term, or administrative.

The experiment was an extremely interesting one from the governmental point of view. The utter lack of competing governmental organs, the plural character of the executive body, its internal organization and the nature and complexity of its tools alike contribute to distinguish it from similar experiments. And, as was the case with the state constitutions in general, the chief value derived from the observation

---

[2] It will be remembered the Maryland council was expressly constituted an administrative board. Its records show that it functioned as such. Archives of Maryland, vols. xvi and xxi.

of the experiment was a negative one. The results obtained were seen to be unsatisfactory. These results were attributed to certain faults of organization. It was these faults that the makers of the Constitution desired to remedy.

Congress was, however, not a static body. By sheer force of necessity there was gradually evolved a method of performing governmental functions quite different from the method adopted at the outset. In the early days of its existence Congress attempted to pass on everything while acting as a corporate whole. Having reached a decision, it entrusted its execution to whatever agency seemed at the moment most convenient, perhaps a committee of its own membership,[3] perhaps a state council or convention,[4] perhaps individuals without official status.[5] Such agencies, having carried out the order in question, immediately lapsed. There was neither plan nor organization. Congress was primarily itself the executive, the administrator.

The first step in governmental development was forced by the increasing complexity of business and the physical inability of Congress to do certain things. This step was the partial transformation of the central body from an active administrator to the enactor of administrative laws for subordinate agencies of a permanent character. That is to say, Congress found itself obliged to set up permanent agencies, to fix their duties by permanent rules, to provide means for

---

[3] For example, the following order: " Resolved. That a committee be appointed for the purpose of borrowing the sum of six thousand pounds, . . . and that the said committee apply the said sum of money to the purchase of gunpowder for the use of the continental army; that the delegates for Pennsylvania compose said committee with power as well to borrow the money as to apply it to the purpose intended " (Secret Journals of Acts and Proceedings of Congress, vol. i, p. 14).

[4] " That the President be desired to write to the powder committees, or committees of safety, in this city and New York . . . to forward to the camp as much gunpowder as they can spare " (ibid., vol. i., p. 22).

[5] " Resolved that . . . ($25,000) be paid by the continental treasurers to Reese Meredith, George Clymer, etc. merchants . . . to be by them applied to the purpose of importing gunpowder " (ibid., vol. i, p. 23).

controlling them in their activities, and to determine their
relations to the only body possessed of original power, itself.

This process was carried out slowly and hesitantly, and
most inadequately. The creation of the office of the commander-in-chief and the preparation of his instructions[6] is
an early example, and a typical one. The active duties of
the office were left entirely uncertain, as were its relations to
the Congress. And, in fact, when the lower offices of the
army were created, especially the commissary-general's and
the quartermaster-general's offices, no attempt was made to
describe their duties at all.[7]

If this had been indicative of a desire on the part of Congress to rid itself of administrative details and to vest ample
powers in the hands of competent administrative or military
officers, there would be little complaint or ground for criticism. Such, of course, was not the case. It was incompetency, not liberality, that determined the lack of system.
Congress was, and remained, conspicuously unwilling to
divest itself of power.

It is for this reason that the administrative agency, acting
under rules set for it by Congress, took the form rather of
the committee of Congress than that of the non-Congressional
office. Certain of the latter were, in fact, created at an early
date, notably the office of treasurer,[8] a purely ministerial
position, and that of postmaster general, to which considerable power of appointment and considerable administrative
discretion was attached.[9] But the committee was the real
seed bed for administrative growth.

We have cited an illustration of the committee acting as
agent to carry out a single order of Congress.[10] There was
another phase of committee activity which deserves notice,
that of investigation of and report on either some single

---

[6] Ibid., vol. i, pp. 17–18.
[7] Journals of Congress (Way and Gideon, 1823), vol. i, p. 84.
[8] Journals of Congress, vol. i, p. 130.
[9] Ibid., vol. i, p. 124.
[10] See above, note 3.

matter or a programme of work.[11]   It was a natural, and probably unconscious, development to combine these two elements of committee activity, to give to the same body that reported a measure the task of carrying it out, to assign other business of the same kind to this same group and to create in that way a permanent body.   Gradually the necessity of at least a degree of systematization was brought home, and the duties of these committees were regulated by permanent ordinances.

A striking illustration of this process is the origin of the Naval Committee.[12]   On October 5th, a committee of three was appointed " to prepare a plan for intercepting two vessels, which are on their way to Canada, laden with arms and powder." [13]   On the 5th and 6th this committee reported, and on the 13th it was decided to fit out " a swift sailing vessel . . . for a cruise of three months," a special committee of three being appointed " to prepare an estimate of the expense and to contract with proper persons to fit out the vessel," while also reporting their opinion on an additional vessel and an estimate of its cost.[14]   On October 30th the report was received, together with additional recommendations, whereupon four members were added to its numbers " to carry into execution with all possible execution as well the resolutions of Congress passed the 13th instant, as those passed this day, for fitting out armed vessels." [15]

This committee, so adventitiously created, became the head of the naval establishment.   In its dual capacity as administrator it reported measures for Congressional consideration, fitted out ships, prepared sailing instructions, functioned, in

---

[11] Thus on May 27, 1775, a committee of six was appointed " to consider on ways and means to supply these colonies with ammunition and military stores." Journals of Congress, vol. i, p. 74. Another " to bring in an estimate of the money necessary to be raised." Ibid., vol. i, p. 79. Another " to prepare rules and regulations for the government of the army." Ibid., vol. i, p. 83.

[12] The following account is condensed from Paullin, Navy of the Revolution, chap. i.

[13] Journals of Congress, vol. i, p. 146.

[14] Ibid., vol. i, pp. 153-154.

[15] Ibid., vol. i, p. 159.

short, as what in fact it really was, an embryonic department of naval affairs,[16] until supplanted by a similar body, the Marine Committee.[17]

No formal ordinance was drafted determining the exact competence of these naval committees, the first enactment of the sort being the ordinance of October 28, 1779, creating the admiralty board.[18]   Nevertheless, isolated resolutions determined its competence from time to time and, taken as a whole, form a body of administrative law for a separate and subordinate administrative organ in a very real sense, for several were general in character in contradistinction to the special orders of earlier times.[19]

There is no need further to follow the details of this interesting development.   Suffice it to say that in the same fashion that the naval committee came into existence, there sprang up other bodies such as the " standing committee of five . . . for superintending the treasury ";[20] the board of war and ordinance, which, despite its title, was only another committee;[21] the medical committee, which throughout the war exercised an independent power of supervision over the hospital service;[22] the " secret committee,"[23] superseded by the commerce committee,[24] which kept in charge the important, and probably lucrative, business of importation of military sup-

---

[16] Paullin, p. 60.

[17] Ibid., p. 87.

[18] Laws of the Thirteen States from 1789 to 1815, vol. i, p. 626. Despite the title, volume i contains a collection of the important ordinances of the old Congress.

[19] For example, the resolution of December 22, 1785, empowering the committee to issue instructions to the commander of the fleet; that of January 25, 1776, specifically placing the direction of the fleet in the naval committee; that of June 6, 1776, empowering the committee to name ships. There are several others. See Laws of the United States, 1789–1815, vol. i, pp. 620–626.

[20] February 17, 1776; Journals of Congress, vol. i, p. 267.

[21] June 12, 1776; ibid., vol. i, pp. 370–371.

[22] September 14, 1775; Ibid., vol. i, p. 140. For its termination see Journals of Congress, vol. iii, p. 626.

[23] September 18, 1775; Secret Journals of Acts and Proceedings of Congress, vol. i, p. 27.

[24] Created July 5, 1777; Journals of Congress, vol. ii, p. 188. Discontinued October 29, 1781; Ibid., vol. iii, p. 682.

plies; and the very important committee of secret correspondence,[25] or, as it was later known, the committee of foreign affairs.

The salient characteristics of this development are apparent. There is, in the first place, an incipient tendency towards specialization of functions which looks towards the
removal of administration, as such, from Congress to other
bodies, leaving to Congress the duties of organization, definition of duties, appropriation and control. On the other
hand, there is a personal fusion of powers, the administrative officers being also members of Congress. From the
fact that these bodies were not only administrative agencies,
but committees, there resulted a continuation of the practice
of permitting them to report not only on individual matters,
but on policies and even administrative laws.

The element of order and system thus introduced should
not be overemphasized. Throughout the whole of the period
of the war minor administrative agencies multiplied with
astounding rapidity. Especially was this true in the service
of supply. There were the commissary general and his deputies, the clothier general, the commissaries of forage, the
commissaries of hides, special committees of Congress to
purchase certain bills of goods, in quite the original style of
doing business, state agencies doing business with continental
funds, etc., etc. It would be futile to attempt to discuss the
relations of these one with another. Everything was confusion, and the confusion was only worse confounded when
Congress sought to effect a cure by introducing further complexity.

Nor did the devolution of a portion of actual administration to other bodies prevent Congress from devoting large
parts of its time to matters which should never have come
before it at all. Even the incomplete indices of the printed

---

[25] Created November 29, 1775; Ibid., vol. i, p. 192. Some of these
committees were formally organized by ordinance at the time of their
creation, while some were not. The distinction is of no particular
practical importance.

Journals list special committee after special committee deal-
ing with individual matters of this kind. Congress, too,
continued until the end to settle matters of minute detail on
its floor, leaving to the administrative agency the ministerial
duty of carrying out each decision as it was reached.

It is common knowledge that this system failed, and failed
lamentably. Inefficiency and waste, if not downright pecu-
lation and corruption, were as sure to follow as the night the
day. In the wake of the inefficiency came discontent, a discontent which seized upon certain features of the system as
the causes of the general administrative debacle, and demanded reformation.

Specifically, three general reforms were asked: personal
separation of powers, unitary departmental control and integration. Over this platform there arose a difference of
opinion which divided Congress, whatever its personnel, into
two continuing schools, the " liberatives " and " constructives "
of Wharton's famous description. The former were the
national counterparts of those opponents of governmental
energy whom we met in the States; the latter correspond to
those political leaders who had struggled in the States for
unitary military control and the executive veto.

It was only by slow degrees that a partial recognition of
these demands was secured. In October, 1777, the Congressional board of war and ordinance was replaced by a board
of three who were not members of Congress,[26] but within a
year two Congressional members were added.[27] In 1779 the
Marine Committee gave way to an admiralty board composed
of two Congressional and three non-Congressional members,[28] and the treasury committee to a similarly constructed
treasury board.[29] Finally, in 1781, the " executives " forced
the issue and won a complete victory. January 10th provision was made for a department of foreign affairs under

---

[26] Journals of Congress, vol. ii, p. 295.
[27] Ibid., vol. iii, p. 105.
[28] Ibid., vol. iii, p. 382.
[29] Ibid., vol. iii, p. 330.

the leadership of a secretary,[30] and a month later the departments of war, of marine and of the treasury were similarly organized.[31]

That these defects which were sought to be remedied were the fundamental cause of the difficulty may well be doubted. The truth was that the internal organization of Congress and its lack of power were even more at fault. It may especially be doubted whether, if there had been a more complete devolution of administrative discretion to the committees and less waste of time by Congress itself, the personal duality of functions might not have proved satisfactory. Be that as it may, the attitude of the " executive " school was definite and comprehensible.

Washington was one of the earliest, as he was one of the most consistent, proponents of the combined ideas. As early as July 10, 1775, he wrote as follows to Congress:

I should be extremely deficient in Gratitude, as well as Justice, if I did not take the first opportunity to acknowledge the Readiness and Attention which the provincial Congress and different Committees have shown to make everything as convenient and agreeable as possible: but there is a vital and inherent Principle of Delay incompatible with military service in transacting Business thro' such numerous and different Channels. I esteem it therefore my Duty to represent the Inconvenience that must unavoidably ensue from dependence on a number of Persons for supplies, and submit it to the Consideration of the Congress whether the publick Service will not be best promoted by appointing a Commissary General for these purposes.[32]

Not only the creation of the general officers of supply, but of the civil office of board of war, were the results of his recommendations,[33] and the great reorganization of 1781 had been strongly recommended by him. Writing to a friend in Congress, he argued as follows:

There are two things, as I have often declared, which, in my

---

[30] Ibid., vol. iii, p. 564.
[31] Ibid., vol. iii, p. 574. The full measure of this gain was not retained, the finance commission being restored May 28, 1784; ibid., vol. iv, p. 421.
[32] Washington to Congress, July 10, 1775; Writings (Ford ed.), vol. iii, p. 12.
[33] Washington to Congress, June 13, 1776; Writings (Ford ed.), vol. iii, p. 139.

opinion, are indispensably necessary to the well-being and good government of our public affairs. These are, greater powers to Congress, and more responsibility and permanency in the executive bodies. . . . If Congress suppose the boards composed of their body and always fluctuating are competent to the great business of war (which requires not only close application, but constant and uniform train of thinking and acting), they will most assuredly deceive themselves.[34]

Robert Morris came early to the same opinion:

If Congress mean to succeed in this contest, they must pay good executive men to do their business as it ought to be done, and not lavish millions away by their own mismanagement. . . . I do aver that there will be more money lost, totally lost in horses, wagons, cattle, etc., for want of sufficient numbers of proper persons to look after them, than would have paid all the salaries Paine ever did or ever will grumble at.[35]

Hamilton at about the same period analyzed the matter in masterly fashion:

Another defect in our system is want of method and energy in the administration. This had partly resulted from the other defect [the weakness of Congress]; but in a great degree from prejudice, and the want of a proper executive. Congress have kept the power too much in their own hands and have meddled too much with details of every sort. Congress is, properly, a deliberative corps, and it forgets itself when it attempts to play the executive. It is impossible such a body. numerous as it is, and constantly fluctuating, can ever act with sufficient decision or with system.

Continuing, he compares the relative merits of boards and departments with single heads, to the great advantage of the latter:

It would give us a chance of more knowledge, more activity, more responsibility, and, of course, more zeal and attention. Boards partake of a part of the inconveniences of larger assemblies. Their decisions are slower, their energy less, their responsibility more diffused. They will not have the same abilities and knowledge as an administration by single men. . . . The members of Boards will take less pains to inform themselves and arrive to eminence, because they have fewer motives to do it. All these reasons conspire to give a preference to the plan of vesting the great executive departments of the State in the hands of individuals. As these men will be, of course, at all times under the direction of Congress, we shall blend the advantages of a monarchy and republic in our constitution.

Nor would this result in reducing the prestige of Congress:

---

[34] Washington to James Duane, December 20, 1780; Bancroft, Formation of the Constitution, vol. i, p. 283.

[35] Oberholtzer, Robert Morris, Patriot and Financier, pp. 34–35.

They would have precisely the same rights and powers as heretofore, happily disencumbered of the detail. They would have to inspect the conduct of their ministers, deliberate upon their plans, originate others for the public good; only observing this rule—that they ought to consult their ministers, and get all the information and advice they could from them, before they entered into any new measures or made changes in the old.[36]

Experience was undoubtedly on the side of the executives. The example of Washington was a host in itself. Energy, probity, disinterestedness, and a magnificent tactfulness in avoiding even the semblance of advancing his personal interests are written large on almost every one of his official acts. His patient devotion to the cause of independence was, time and time again, the sole support on which it rested. Fear of the "man on horseback" should have seemed rather puerile in the face of practical experience, and especially after the dignified and patently sincere retirement to Mount Vernon, and the even more striking illustration of entire absence of selfish purpose afforded by the Newburgh episode.

What was even more important, Washington afforded the country an example of the national leader *par excellence*. In the troubled days that followed peace, thoughts of how his personality had ridden the storm of separatism and failure recurred, with the inevitable conclusion that it was only through the same agency that orderly government could be restored.[37]

But Washington's was not an isolated instance of the value of the efficient and responsible executive head. The example of the first Commissary General, Joseph Trumbull, is an eloquent testimonial to the efficacy of this principle of administration, and an equally eloquent illustration of the way in which Congress mismanaged business.

---

[36] Hamilton to James Duane, September 3, 1780; Hamilton, Works (Lodge ed.), vol. i, pp. 209–210.

[37] See Knox to Washington, January 14, 1787; Correspondence of the Revolution (Sparks ed.), vol. iv, p. 156. Knox urges Washington not to attend the Convention, because "there may, indeed, arise some solemn occasion, in which you may conceive it to be your duty again to exert your utmost talents to promote the happiness of your country." Just what Knox meant is conjectural, but his state of mind is interesting.

The following report, signed by two such conspicuous anti-executives as Samuel Adams and Richard Henry Lee, speaks for itself:

It appears to your committee that the late commissary-general Joseph Trumbull, coming into office in the earliest stage of the American contest, found himself without a system by which to trace the plan of his duty; that with great care, industry, labor, and attention, he instituted a plan by which the army, during his continuance in office, was amply supplied, with much economy, and to general satisfaction: that, during his commissariate, he was obliged to act not only in capacity of commissary-general of purchases, but to direct all the issues of provisions, and for near two campaigns, had the additional duty of purveyor of the hospitals and quartermaster general; . . . it appears also to your committee, that the said commissary-general made great savings to the public by his large and seasonable purchases and contracts, outrunning and anticipating, in many instances, the orders of Congress, by which means he kept up large supplies, thereby moderating the demands of the seller, intercepting monopolies, and keeping down prices which are now greatly augmented.[38]

And yet Congress, through its short-sighted policy of keeping power within its own hands, drove Trumbull from office. John Marshall's account of the proceeding follows:

The principle adopted in the new arrangement which expelled Colonel Trumbull from the service, if an error, is one which an assembly, without that practical knowledge which is drawn from experience, will ever be much inclined to commit. It was a creation, in some of the subordinate offices, of an independence on the head of the department, and an immediate and direct dependence on Congress. In addition to the commissary-general of purchases, and a commissary-general of issues, each to be appointed by Congress, the new plan contemplated four deputies in each department, who were also to be appointed by the same body, and were not removeable by the head of the department, but might be suspended and accused before Congress, who should then examine the charge, and either remove the accused individual from his office, or restore him to it.

This *imperium in imperio*, erected in direct opposition to the opinion of the commander-in-chief, effectually drove Colonel Trumbull from the army. In his letter to Congress, dated the nineteenth of July, 1777, stating his reasons for declining the commission of commissary-general of purchases, which was offered him, he says, 'In my humble opinion, the head of every department ought to have control of it. In this establishment, an *imperium in imperio* is created. If I consent to act, I must be at continual variance with the whole department, and of course be in continual hot water. I must turn accuser, and be continually applying to Congress, and attending with witnesses, to support my charges; or I must sit down in ease and quiet, let the deputies do as they like, and enjoy a sinecure. . . . I

---

[38] Journals of Congress, vol. iii, p. 239.

can by no means consent to act under a regulation, which, in my opinion, will never answer the purpose intended by Congress, nor supply the army as it should be.[39]

The results of this were not slow in coming. "In every military division of the continent, loud complaints were made of the deficiency of supplies," and it is interesting to observe that in less than a year Congress found it necessary to recede from its position in order to obtain a competent man. Included in its reorganization ordinance was the provision that "the commissary-general of purchases have full power to appoint and remove every officer in his department."[40] It is equally interesting to note that this same Wadsworth, who then dictated his own terms to Congress, as representative from Connecticut in the first Congress, came forward as the chief defender of the principle of the unit head of the treasury department and of the financial administration of Robert Morris.[41] The lessons of Revolutionary experience, written in terms of human suffering, were not soon forgotten.

The later ordinances of Congress respecting the departments indicate an increasing adherence to the principles of good administrative organization. Thus when the War Department was reorganized in 1782, a notable degree of integration was secured by a provision that the clothier general should "receive his instructions from the war office, and that the distributions of clothing for the army be made under the secretary of war's directions," that "the commissary general of prisoners, as far as respects the securing of military prisoners, and making returns of them, take his directions from the secretary of war," and that "all military and other officers attending upon, or connected with, the army of the

---

[39] Marshall, Life of Washington, vol. ii, pp. 299–300.

[40] Journals of Congress, vol. iii, p. 511.

[41] Annals of Congress, first Congress, first session, vol. i, pp. 404–406. The debate throws much light on the conflicting forces in the struggle over the departments. Cf. Boudinot's remark on Morris's administration: "He remembered one hundred and forty-six supernumerary officers were brushed off in one day, who had long been sucking the vital blood and spirit of the nation." Annals of Congress, vol. i, p. 410.

United States be, and they are hereby, required and enjoined to observe the directions of the secretary of war in making and transmitting proper returns, and such other matters as may tend to facilitate the business of his department." [42] In that of January 27, 1785, it was expressly provided that the secretary should "appoint and remove, at pleasure, all persons employed under him, and [should] be responsible for their conduct in office." [43] Also, when the business of Indian affairs was finally regulated in 1786, the superintendents were required to correspond with Congress only through the Secretary of War and to "obey all instructions which they shall, from time to time, receive from the said secretary of war." [44] Similarly, in the act creating the office of superintendent of finance, that officer was empowered "to direct and control all persons employed in procuring supplies for the public service, and in the expenditure of public money." [45]

Nor did the insistence on the principle of personal separation of powers which had finally put the departments under non-Congressional heads break all organic connection between Congress and the departments. Congress, of course, remained in the relation of supreme head to all other national agencies, and continued to be the source of administrative power. It still determined the number and functions of all officers, and was free to issue specific orders when it saw fit, while always exercising the general right of control. But the original committee origin of the departments left its impress on them when they ceased to be a part of Congress.

The secretary of foreign affairs was required to "report on all cases expressly referred to him for that purpose by Congress, and on all others touching his department, in which he may conceive it necessary," being also empowered to attend all sessions of Congress and to "give information

---

[42] Ordnance of April 10, 1782; Journals of Congress, vol. ix, pp. 8–9. The last clause had been included in the ordinance of October 17, 1777; Journals of Congress, vol. ii, p. 295.
[43] Journals of Congress, vol. iv, p. 462.
[44] Ibid., vol. iv, p. 678.
[45] Ibid., vol. iii, p. 575.

to Congress respecting his department, explain and answer objections to his reports when under consideration, if required by a member and no objection be made by Congress," and to "answer such inquiries respecting his department as may be put from the chair by order of Congress, and to questions stated in writing, about matters of fact which lie within his knowledge, when put by the president at the request of a member, and not disapproved of by Congress." [46] The secretary of war was "to give his opinion on all such subjects as shall be referred to him by Congress; and if, at any time, he shall think a measure necessary, to which his powers are incompetent, he shall communicate the same to Congress, for their direction therein." [47] The superintendent of finance was "to digest and report plans for improving and regulating the finances, and for establishing order and economy in the expenditure of the public money." [48]

As a matter of fact, after the cessation of hostilities had relieved the national government of the most of its administrative business, the administrative organs themselves seemed to have been regarded as satisfactorily organized. Knox wrote, when accepting the secretaryship of war:

Congress have rendered the powers and duties of the office respectable.[49]

To the same effect Otto, the French representative in America, declared in 1787:

The various departments have been arranged in the most perfect manner; a regular system has been introduced into all the branches of the general administration, and, but for the want of permanent revenue, the United States would be one of the best organized of governments.[50]

---

[46] Ordinance of February 22, 1782; Journals of Congress, vol. iii, p. 723.

[47] Ordinance of April 10, 1782; ibid., vol. iv, pp. 8–9.

[48] Ordinance of February 7, 1781; ibid., vol. iii, p. 575.

[49] Knox to Washington, March 24, 1785; Correspondence of the Revolution (Sparks ed.), vol. iv, p. 98.

[50] Otto to Vergennes, February 10, 1787; Bancroft, Formation of the Constitution, vol. ii, p. 411. Cited in Learned, President's Cabinet, p. 58. Professor Learned thinks, without doubt correctly, that as Congress declined, Robert Morris and Jay "probably exercised large if not directive influence over it" (p. 57), and that John Jay "became really what may be called the chief executive of the Con-

There was, however, no constitutional possibility of erecting a legal barrier which Congress could not at pleasure cross. As a consequence there was no method by which Congress could be prevented from continuing to busy itself with details, to take up departmental matters that came before it from any source and to assign their consideration to special committees without consultation with the departmental head. In foreign affairs, this irregular method of procedure was the subject of a vigorous and successful complaint by Jay, with the result that Congress required all correspondence to and from Congress on the subject of foreign relations to pass through the secretary's hands.[51]　But Congress refused to stay within the bounds of what properly was its business, and until the end continued to act as an administrative body, as almost any page of its recorded proceedings will demonstrate.

It will have been noticed that practically all the progress made prior to 1787 was in the direction of a personal separation of functions or of internal administrative organization. The question of an independent executive department could hardly be raised under the existing frame of government. Nothing, in fact, was suggested along these lines except Jefferson's proposed Committee of States. Accordingly governmental experience, except for this, failed to suggest a solution of the complex question of a distribution of functions into the two classes, legislative and executive.

---

federation" (p. 58). This conclusion confirms one main thesis of the present study, that the presidency was an indigenous product. It will be shown, however, that the office was derived more directly from an imitation of the New York governorship than as a result of this process.

[51] Journals of Congress, vol. iv, p. 468. See too Monroe to Madison, February 1, 1785, Monroe, Writings, vol. i, pp. 61–62 and Madison's reply, Madison, Writings (Hunt ed.), vol. ii, p. 127. Among other things, Madison declares: "The practice of Congress during the administration of his predecessor was never fixed, and frequently improper." This testimony is important, because the journals often fail to show the exact manner in which business first came before Congress. See a similar resolution on Indian affairs, July 18, 1787, Journals of Congress, vol. iv, p. 756.

This experiment of Jefferson's is of interest, first because of its failure. It was a final blow, if one were needed, to executive plurality. The experience of the committee was ludicrous in the extreme. The New England delegates became angered because the Southerners desired to adjourn over Saturdays "for the benefit of their health and because they have not been accustomed to do business on that day" or, the irate Massachusetts writer adds, "any other day"; one member in the course of a debate "rose and halooed as tho' he might be heard through town"; another told the secretary to enter a certain resolution "at his peril." The upshot was that two members left, breaking the quorum, lamenting as they went that "such men [as their opponents] are unfit to govern this country." In charity be it said that it is reported that the heat was "intense."[52]

But the greater interest lies in the causes that led Jefferson to insist upon it, and especially in the catalogue of executive duties with which he felt it desirable to endow the committee. These reasons were fully expressed in the following letter written, it should be noted, prior to the rising of the Federal Convention:

I think it very material to separate in the hands of Congress the Executive and Legislative powers, as the judiciary already are in some degree. This I hope will be done. The want of it has been the source of more evil than we have experienced from any other cause. Nothing is so embarrassing as the details of execution. The smallest trifle of that kind occupies as long as the most important act of legislation, and takes place of everything else. Let any man recollect, or look over the files of Congress, he will observe the most important propositions hanging over from week to week and month to month, till the occasion have past them and the thing never done. I have ever viewed the executive details as the greatest cause of evil to us, because they in fact place us as if we had no federal head, by diverting the attention of that head from great to small objects; and should this division of power not be recommended by the Convention, it is my opinion Congress should make it itself by establishing an executive committee.[53]

---

[52] Dunn to Gerry, July 20, 1784; Austin, Life of Elbridge Gerry, vol. i, pp. 441–447.

[53] Jefferson to Carrington, August 4, 1787; Writings (Ford ed.), vol. iv, p. 424.

This from the man who, under the influence of intense indignation at the abuses of the old regime in France, was at practically the same time condoning the Shay men of Massachusetts, was a concession of significance. It shows that in national as well as state government a separate executive department was demanded by the exigencies of efficient government, until it became a foregone conclusion that any new scheme of government would include such an organ.

The degree of power with which Jefferson wished to endow the committee is worthy of special notice. By article ten of the Articles, national powers requiring the vote of nine States could not be exercised by the committee, but all others might be vested in it by Congress. These prohibited powers included the making of war, the granting of letters of marque, the making of treaties or alliances, coining money or regulating its value, ascertaining sums necessary for welfare or defence, emitting bills, borrowing money, appropriating money, agreeing on the number of land or sea forces or of war vessels, or appointing a commander-in-chief. To these prohibitions Jefferson would have added the sending and receiving ambassadors, the establishment of rules of decision in case of captures, or the establishment of courts of appeal for their trial, the determination of interstate disputes, and the fixing of standards.[54]

Positively, however, he would give to this body " for conducting the business of the United States " the following important functions:

Determination of specific private claims to soil under the general rule, regulation of Indian trade and management of Indian affairs, regulation of the post-office, appointment of military officers, save the commander-in-chief and regimental officers, and of all naval officers, commissioning all officers, making rules and regulations for the military forces, subject to the Congressional Article of War, the building, buying and equipping of ships decided on by Congress, the actual making

[54] Draft Report for Committee of States, Writings (Ford ed.), vol. iii, p. 390.

of requisitions, "superintending all officers appertaining to the United States," "directing and controlling the application of money in the detail according to the general appropriation previously made by Congress, making recess appointments, executing in general the resolutions, orders and ordinances of Congress," and calling extra sessions, all, of course, subject to the law.

It is impossible to say whether Jefferson would have gone farther had it been constitutionally possible. But it should be noted that the trend of national development was towards a superintending administrative agency standing between the departments and Congress. Evidently the frequent assertion that administration in the modern sense was not considered as an executive function is incorrect. The impetus for a separate executive so far as national affairs was concerned was furnished primarily by the desire to free Congress from the necessity of concerning itself with the details of administrative business.[55]

The strictly administrative phase of Congressional action was, of course, not the whole of it. It exercised the great non-legislative powers of appointment, of determining financial policy, and of control of foreign affairs as well. Its incapacity in all three lines of endeavor is too well known to require demonstration. Factional differences kept important offices unfilled for long periods. Time and again purely

---

[55] Compare with this attempt Hamilton's criticism of the existing system in his resolutions for a general convention adopted by the New York legislatrue in 1783. A main division of the points in which it was declared defective was: "in confounding legislative and executive powers in a single body: as, that of determining on the number and quantity of force, land and naval, to be employed for the common defence, and of directing their operations when raised and equipped, with that of ascertaining and making requisitions for the necessary sums or quantities of money to be paid by the respective States into the common treasury; contrary to the most approved and well-founded maxims of free government, which require that the legislative, executive, and judicial authorities should be deposited in distinct and separate hands." Hamilton, Works (Lodge ed.), vol. i, p. 289. Hamilton's inclusion of the determination of the budget and of the number of armed forces as executive functions is especially significant.

personal considerations proved the governing factor in determination of foreign policy. The laborious efforts to draft instructions for the negotiators of the treaty of peace with the accompanying intrigues of the French faction against the English faction served to prove Congress as incompetent in this capacity as in its strictly administrative character. By 1787 it was a thoroughly discredited body.

Thus in many ways national experience duplicated the teachings of state experience. We find the same conclusions that executive efficiency and responsibility vary inversely in proportion to the size of the executive body; that the power to appoint and remove subordinates is essential to control and responsibility on the part of the real head; that military efficiency is directly dependent on unification of command; and that a legislative body should not concern itself with the details of administration.

The adoption of the principle of separation of powers, as interpreted to mean the exercise of different functions of government by departments officered by entirely different individuals, also seemed insistently demanded as a *sine qua non* of governmental efficiency. It seemed, indeed, the only way to secure that functional distribution, that wresting of non-legislative powers from a body that ought to be entirely legislative, which was so greatly desired. It gave point and meaning to the statements of the two theorists whose influence was so great, Blackstone and Montesquieu, that confusion of powers in the same hands was tyranny.

And yet there is a real difference between the solutions towards which the two kinds of experience seemed to point. In national affairs, the separate executive, so far as one had evolved, had come into being under the law. National executive power was inherently and unavoidably subordinate to the legislative. Executive organs depended for the determination of their powers on the law; they were strictly the creatures of the law. The next step in order after the creation of Jefferson's committee, had it been possible to take it, would have been the creation of a committee of one, which still would have acted under Congress. In short, the tendency in the national field was more towards separation than equality. It remained to be seen how the new frame of government would settle the matter; how, particularly, it would work out the relations of the existing departments, creatures of the law, to the executive chief. Many characteristics of the new executive were predetermined, but not this, the most vital of all.

CHAPTER IV

THE PRESIDENCY IN THE FEDERAL CONVENTION

Having established the fact that the political psychology
of the men who framed the Federal Constitution was by no
means characterized by that jealousy of the executive which
was so prevalent in 1776, and that, indeed, the pendulum of
conservative opinion had swung so far in the opposite direction that the "people's representatives" had become the chief
object of its dislike, and having seen that the desirability of
certain principles of executive organization had been deeply
impressed on the conservative mind by actual experience with
government, it will be well to attempt to visualize the problem
of national executive power as it appeared to the delegates
in 1787.

In the largest sense of the term, it appeared the chief and
the most difficult problem to be solved. The fundamental
defect of the existing national government was lack of power,
not lack of functions. As Publius claimed, "if the new
Constitution be examined with accuracy and candour it will
be found that the change which it proposes consists much
less in the addition of NEW POWERS to the Union, than
in 'the invigoration of its ORIGINAL POWERS."[1]   Even
the vesting of the national organization with the taxing power
was but a substitution of new means for old. The field of
commerce was indeed almost the only completely new function that the national government would acquire. This, with
the important prohibitions on the States, was the only substantive change to be made. The rest was a matter of ma-
chinery. The Federal Convention did its work much in the
same spirit of, for example, those British Parliaments which
by slow degrees perfected the mechanical device of *habeas
corpus.*

---

[1] Federalist Papers, No. 45 (Lodge ed.), p. 291.

The most far reaching of these mechanistic changes was the substitution of direct action of the national government on the individual for the existing method. It required no peculiar clairvoyance to perceive that this meant the substitution of national executive officers and national courts for those of the States in exactly the proportion that nationalism was achieved.

The executive problem was thus primarily one of law enforcement, the institution of a department well enough equipped with power to see to it that the laws were faithfully executed in distant Georgia and individualistic western Pennsylvania and western Massachusetts as well as in the commercial centers of the seaboard. When the extent of the territory for which the new government was to make laws is considered, multiplied many times as it was by poor transportation facilities, the problem takes on almost the character of a problem of imperial administration. Theorists were as one in confining feasible democratic government to small areas, in view of the superior executive efficiency of governments containing a large proportion of executive irresponsibility and the universal belief that a republican executive was inherently weak.[2] The delegates' chief concern was thus to secure an executive strong enough, not one weak enough. To do this they believed, and rightly, was peculiarly difficult and complex.

The fact that certain principles of executive organization

---

[2] See for example Hamilton's famous speech where he declared that it was generally admitted that it was not possible to secure a really good republican executive. Farrand, Records, vol. i, p. 289. He used quite different language when defending the Constitution. See Federalist Papers, No. 9. The friends of the Constitution were at much pains to answer this objection, utilizing fully, if not very honestly, Montesquieu's statement concerning confederate republics. See Montesquieu, Spirit of Laws, bk. ix, chap. 1. Montesquieu had something in mind quite different from the type of government the Constitution erected, as may be observed from Hamilton's omissions from the quotation in Federalist Papers No. 9, namely, the examples which Montesquieu cited of what he meant. For Montesquieu's argument concerning the superior executive strength found in monarchies, see Spirit of Laws, bk. v, chap. x, whose title is "On the Expedition Peculiar to the Executive Power in Monarchies."

had become fixed in the conservative mind did not, it may well be repeated, predetermine the nature of the national executive. Not only were there the two separate lines of development, in State and nation respectively, with a fundamental difference between them on an all-important point, but there were delegates at Philadelphia who had not undergone the whole of the conservative reaction. It will be remembered that in introducing the discussion of the general tendencies of conservative thought a caveat was entered against interpreting general opinion as unanimous opinion.[3] While the opinion of the class as a whole was under consideration, minority opinion could be disregarded. But this is no longer true where the activities of a small group from this class are concerned. Then personal differences become of momentous importance.

It is not very easy to differentiate the delegates into classes solely on the basis of their adherence to a strong executive or a weak. There were other divisions, frequently more fundamental, whose lines cut across those which concern our investigation. Chief of these was that which separated the members into small state and large state groups. There was a further division, based on social and economic grounds, between the North and the South, and especially between the North and the three southernmost States. In addition, a State might well have peculiar internal problems which influenced its attitude. Such, for example, was the case with South Carolina, where the conservatives controlled the state legislature, though outnumbered by the newcomers of the interior. The executive was wholly the product of no one of these influences, but rather of the checking of one interest by another, the counterchecking of each by a third.

However, if " strong executive " be substituted for " monarchy," the following analysis of Luther Martin,[4] which, though a part of a campaign document, has the advantage of

---

[3] See above, chap. i, p. 14.
[4] Luther Martin, Genuine Information ; Farrand, Records, vol. iii, p. 172, et seq.

being from the pen of a participant, furnishes a fairly accurate description of parties in the Convention.

There were three parties, he said. The first was that "whose object and wish it was to abolish and annihilate all State governments, and to bring forward one general government, over this extensive continent, of a monarchical nature, under certain restrictions and limitations." The second "was not for the abolition of the State governments, nor for the introduction of a monarchical government under any form; but they wished to establish such a system as could give their own States undue power and influence in the government over the other States." The third, the truly federal party, as Martin viewed the situation, "were for proceeding upon terms of *federal equality;* they were for taking our present federal system as the basis of their proceedings." It was a coalition of the first two groups that carried the Constitution, he continued, the large state delegates with state sovereignty proclivities abandoning their state sovereignty ideas in return for the enhancement of large state power.

Like most attempts at generalization, Martin's explanation is open to much, and valid, criticism. It contains for present purposes, however, a sufficient approximation of the truth. Nationalism and adherence to a strong executive did go hand in hand, as he said. Also there were large state delegates with pronounced leanings toward state sovereignty and weak government. Where Martin was farthest afield was in lumping all the state delegates into a single class. At the time of the great crisis over representation, Dickinson told Madison:

> You see the consequences of pushing things too far. Some of the members from the small States wish for two branches in the General Legislature, and are friends to a good National Government.[5]

But, he added, equality of representation was a *sine qua non* for small state entrance into the new union. Similarly

---

[5] Farrand, Records, vol. i, p. 255. Madison's note.

Charles Pinckney on the Convention floor declared without contradiction:

> The whole comes to this. Give N. Jersey an equal vote, and she will dismiss her scruples and concur in the valid system.[6]

It was only because enough of the small state representatives were, as Dickinson said, "friends to a good National Government" that the executive department assumed its final shape. We shall see, though, that they demanded their *quid pro quo* before they would "dismiss their scruples."

We have said that for "adherents of monarchy" in Martin's description the term "adherents of a strong executive" should be substituted. It is with considerable trepidation that one doubts a conclusion of Professor Channing, who strongly intimates an opinion that where there was so much smoke about monarchy there must have been some fire, and that the Bishop of Osnaburg rumor probably had some substantial foundation in fact.[7] Surely there was no lack of monarchic talk and, indeed, monarchic sentiment, enough to give a far better foundation for Jefferson's subsequent accusations against the Federalists than Federalist historians have ever been willing to admit.[8] The difficulty really hinges on the definition of monarchy. If monarchy means only an hereditary executive, as Hamilton, for example, claimed,[9] and it is difficult to say that it means anything else, there was, we believe, no really monarchical party in the Convention. As Ezra Stiles recorded in his diary, on the authority of Baldwin, delegate from Georgia, it did not "appear that any members in Convention has the least Idea of insiduously layg the Founda of a future Monarchy like the European or

---

[6] Ibid., vol. i, p. 242.

[7] Channing, History of the United States, vol. iii, pp. 474-475, and references there cited.

[8] See Randall, Life of Jefferson, vol. i, p. 566 ff., for a collection of contemporary statements that a sentiment for monarchy existed.

[9] Farrand, Records, vol. i, p. 290. "Is this a Republican Govt., it will be asked? Yes, in it all the Magistrates are appointed, and vacancies are filled by the people, or a process of election originating with the people." Cf. Dickinson's statement, vol. i, pp. 86-87.

Asiatic Monarchies either antient or modern." [10]   But with this should be coupled Gerry's statement in the Convention that if general public opinion were not to be taken into account, as Madison had argued, a limited monarchy, if regarded as desirable, should be recommended, " tho' the genius of the people were decidedly averse to it." [11]

Desiring a thing abstractly and seeking to obtain it are, however, very different matters.   Also, after all, the finished document had to be ratified before promulgation.   This fact was a mighty weapon in breaking down even the walls of secrecy and isolation which the Convention erected around itself and letting in the influence of that more general public opinion, whose tenets were not those which the Convention approved.

The fact that the work of the Convention had for its subject matter a set of resolutions introduced by Governor Randolph of Virginia, but chiefly the work of James Madison, creates a peculiar interest in the views of the latter concerning executive power on the eve of the Convention.   Madison has with much justice been called the father of the Constitution.   But the claims entered for his paternity do not extend to the fundamentals of Article II.

The truth is that Madison's views on executive power were extremely vague when he came to Philadelphia in 1787.   He realized that the Virginia constitution had created a state of affairs that was undesirable, as is evidenced by notes which he prepared in 1784 for a speech to be delivered on the question of a general revision of that instrument.   The executive department was too weak.   It was dependent on the legislature for its salary and " for character in the triennial expulsion."   It was expensive and might be for life.   Also there was " no mode of expounding constitution and of course no check to Genl. Assembly."   In general, the " Constitution,

---

[10] Farrand, Records, vol. iii, p. 169.
[11] Ibid., vol. i, p. 215.   It may be inferred from Madison's note that Gerry thought constitutional monarchy the ideal of many members, though not necessarily his own.

if so to be called defective in a Union of powers which is tyranny. Montesq." [12]

Two years later, in developing his ideas concerning constitutional government for the benefit of a Kentucky friend, he wrote as follows concerning the executive department:

> Though it claims the 2nd place [that is, in Madison's order of treatment] is not in my estimation entitled to it by its importance, all the great powers which are properly executive being transferred to the federal government. I have made up no final opinion whether the first magistrate should be chosen by the Legislature or the people at large or whether the power should be vested in one man assisted by a council of which the President shall be only primus inter pares. There are examples of each in the U. States and probably advantages and disadvantages attending each. It is material I think that the number of members should be small and that their salaries should be either unalterable by the Legislature or alterable only in such manner as will not affect any individual in place. Our Executive is the worst part of a bad Constitution. The members of it are dependent on the Legislature not only for their wages but for their reputation and 'therefore are not likely to withstand usurpations of that branch. They are besides too numerous and expensive. Their organization vague and perplexed and to crown the absurdity some of the members may without new appointment continue in office for life contrary to one of the Articles of the Declaration of Rights.[13]

He was, in addition, heartily in favor of the New York Council of Revision, " as a further security against fluctuating and undigested laws," and wrote favorably of an independent committee whose function it would be to prepare bills on such subjects as seemed proper to them for submission to the legislature and also to act as a drafting bureau for the legislature when in session.[14]

The real truth of the situation appears from these recommendations. Madison saw the defects of what existed, but he did not as clearly see the remedies. On the fundamental matter of method of choice he was still undecided, and on the equally important matter of unity. Where the makers of the New York constitution had seen the unit executive, Madison saw a " small number." This is an accurate measure of the differences between them. It is certain that Mad-

---

[12] Madison, Writings (Hunt ed.), vol. ii, p. 54, note 1.
[13] Madison to Caleb Wallace, August 23, 1785; Madison, Writings (Hunt ed.), vol. ii, pp. 169-170.
[14] Madison, Writings (Hunt ed.), vol. ii, p. 168.

ison completely understood and approved the theory of limited government. His wholehearted acceptance of the idea of the council of revision indicates an approval of the idea of independent departments. But as yet he did not think the matter through as consistently as had been done by others.

It may be that to Madison's contemplative, unassertive mind the executive problem was not particularly attractive. It may be, and probably is, true that his attention was engrossed in the federal aspects of the problem, for his memorandum on Confederations is the evidence of much laborious effort.[15] At any rate, whatever the reason, his ideas on the subject of executive power were no more complete in 1787 than in 1785. With that intellectual honesty which was always characteristic of the man, he admitted the vagueness with entire candor. Thus, in a letter to Washington, written as late as April 16, 1787, he frankly states:

I have scarcely ventured as yet to form my own opinion either of the manner in which [the executive] ought to be constituted or of the authorities with which it ought to be cloathed.[16]

He still advocates a council of revision, but now "including the great ministerial officers," rather than a portion of the judiciary, and also national appointment of all executive officers, in order to secure real national supremacy. But this is the extent of his positive suggestions.

It should, in justice to Madison, be said that the Virginia resolutions which were submitted by Randolph to the Convention must have been considered by him entirely tentative. An analysis of their executive provisions reveals, however, that they coincide very generally with his ideas so far as they had been formulated. Complete legislative and executive separation, so far as concerns persons, was provided by a resolution prohibiting members of either branch of the legislature from holding other office, State or national, during

---

[15] Of Ancient and Modern Confederacies; Writings (Hunt ed.), vol. ii, pp. 369–390.
[16] Madison to Washington, April 16, 1787; Writings (Hunt ed.), vol. ii, p. 348.

their term of office or — years thereafter. The number of the
chief magistracy was undetermined. Election should be by
the legislature, without eligibility for reëlection. Executive
salaries.should be fixed. A council of revision of the New
York type was provided, which should possess a qualified
veto on national legislation and the proposed legislative veto
of State enactments. The executive powers were to be "to
execute the national laws" and to "enjoy the Executive
rights vested in Congress by the Confederation." [17]

What Madison considered these executive rights to be becomes more apparent from certain supplementary resolutions
introduced by him on June 1. As a substitute for the original definition he moved:

> That a national Executive ought to be constituted with power to
> carry into effect the national laws, to appoint to offices in cases not
> otherwise provided for, and to execute such other powers not Legis-
> lative nor Judiciary in their nature as may from time to time be dele-
> gated by the national Legislature.[18]

Considering the two sets of resolutions as a whole, we may
say that the executive proposed by them was essentially subordinate to the legislature. The fixed nature of the executive salary, the provision for ineligibility for reëlection, and
the council of revision point unmistakably towards a desire
for an independent exercise of the executive powers. But
legislative election and legislative determination of the major
part of executive competency negated any idea of departmental coördination. Madison seems, indeed, to have been
thinking chiefly in terms of the existing national organization.
His executive would have been a smaller committee of States,
strengthened by the veto power, but confined to the business
of carrying out the laws. The influence of state experience
is shown in the salary and the council of revision provisions,
but the primary influence was the national one. Had these
provisions been incorporated into the finished Constitution,

---

[17] Resolutions proposed by Mr. Randolph in Convention, nos. 4, 7,
and 8. Judges were to be chosen by the legislature; resolution 9.
Farrand, Records, vol. i, pp. 20–21.
[18] Ibid., vol. i, p. 67.

the American executive must have been of a type resembling in many fundamental ways the executive of modern Switzerland.

As soon as the executive provisions of the Virginia plan were reached, however, a very different solution for the executive problem was offered by James Wilson of Pennsylvania. A nationalist of the nationalists, he conceived the executive as a part of a governmental whole, which, deriving its powers from the general body of the nation, would supplant separatism and reduce the States to a position of practical and legal subordination to the nation. " If we are to establish a national Government," he said, " that Government ought to flow from the people at large." [19]

With respect to the executive, this meant, negatively, the elimination of the interposition of the States in its composition. Positively, it meant an executive which, resting on the support of the whole people, would maintain its independence against the legislature and so, whatever the emergency, exercise its powers without fear of interference by temporary whims of the people or the people's representatives.

The concrete provisions of Wilson's plan were well calculated to attain these ends. The chief magistracy should be possessed by one man, " as giving most energy, dispatch, and responsibility." [20] Also, this unity must be real, not nominal. There should be no council, " which oftener serves to cover than prevent malpractices." [21] That independence might be real, he proposed an absolute veto, to be vested in a council of revision of the New York type.[22] Most important of all,

---

[19] Ibid., vol. i, p. 151. See further pp. 49, 52, 132. It is not within the scope of the present study to discuss the matter of the Convention's intentions concerning the States' relations to the Union. Men like Wilson and Gouverneur Morris, however, undoubtedly saw with clear vision the necessity of destroying the States qua States, in the strict sense of the word, and understood what they were doing. As Morris said, he could not see how there could be two sovereigns, p. 43.

[20] Ibid., vol. i, p. 65.

[21] Ibid., vol. i, p. 97.

[22] Ibid., vol. i, p. 98.

election should be by the people, and, since no responsibility was owed to them, there should be unlimited reëligibility and a relatively short term.[23]

"He was almost unwilling," Wilson said, "to declare the mode which he wished to take place, being apprehensive that it might appear chimerical. He would say, however, at least that in theory he was for an election by the people; Experience, particularly in N. York and Massts., shewed that all election of the first magistrate by the people at large, was both a convenient and successful mode. The objects of choice in such cases must be persons whose merits have general notoriety." [24]

And again:

Mr. Wilson renewed his declarations in favor of an appointment by the people. ·He wished to derive not only both branches of the Legislature from the people, without the intervention of the State Legislatures but the Executive also, in order to make them independent as possible of each other, as well as of the States.[25]

Evidently, however, the force of anti-democratic sentiment was too strong, and on the ensuing day he moved for election by an electoral college chosen directly by the people.[26]

As to the powers of this officer, Wilson was in accord with the general view that the British prerogative powers were not the proper model, since some were undoubtedly of a legislative nature. The only powers he conceived strictly executive, he said, were "those of executing the laws and appointing officers, not appertaining to and appointed by the Legislature," [27] though he would have extended the appointing power to include appointments to judicial office, since "experience showed the impropriety of such appointments by numerous bodies," the "necessary consequence" of which would be "intrigue, partiality, and concealment." "A principal reason for unity in the Executive," he added, "was

[23] Ibid., vol. i, p. 68.
[24] Ibid., vol. i, p. 68.
[25] Ibid., vol. i, p. 69.
[26] Ibid., vol. i, p. 80.
[27] Ibid., vol. i, pp. 65–66.

that officers might be appointed by a single responsible person." [28]

By accepting the principle of Madison's supplementary resolutions defining executive power, which he seconded, Wilson laid himself liable to the same criticism that Madison did.   But nevertheless Wilson's plan went far beyond Madison's not only on questions of detail such as whether the executive should name the judges, as Wilson believed, or the Senate as Madison preferred,[29] or whether the executive's veto should be absolute, but in general scope.   Choice by the people was the keystone of his concept.   If the president were to be in a position of independence such as he desired, he must be backed by popular support, he must be the representative of the whole people and he must have in his own hands, supported by the authority of the judiciary, a weapon for the protection of his powers, and, we may believe, the power of patronage further to strengthen his position.   The elimination of legislative choice and the ministerial council, with all its potentialities,[30] amounted to a complete revision of the Virginia plan.   If accepted, the new plan would place the executive in a relation of equality to the legislature, since both would derive their powers from the same source and on the same terms, and both would be responsible alike to the voters.

Wilson's appeal to the experience of New York and Massachusetts in support of the principle of popular election, and his insistence "that he was not governed by the British Model which was inapplicable to the situation of this Country, the extent of which was so great, and the manners so republican, that nothing but a great confederated Republic would do for it " [31] are scarcely necessary to indicate where he derived his

---

[28] Ibid., vol. i, p. 119.

[29] Ibid., vol. i, p. 133.

[30] Madison at this stage accepted the idea of a single executive with a council from whose advice he could depart " at his peril " and a long term. See King's notes, Farrand, Records, vol. i, p. 70.

[31] In the debate on unity or plurality of the executive. Farrand, Records, vol. i, p. 66.

ideas. He was thinking of the only strong and satisfactory republican executive in existence, the New York governorship. The experiences of Massachusetts were corroborative, but the inclusion of the council of revision and the elimination of the privy council put the New York stamp unmistakably on these recommendations. Even the term which was recommended, three years, was that of the New York governor.

The immediate results of Wilson's activities were relatively slight, being confined to the matter of unity. The issue was clear cut, Wilson declaring in advance that he intended to have no council,[32] and the vote was decisive, seven States to three, New York, Delaware and Maryland furnishing the dissent.[33] For the rest, however, the principles of the Virginia plan were retained. Choice by electors was defeated by a large vote, and legislative election retained by a similar one.[34] The term of office was set at seven years, the principle of ineligibility being retained. The chief magistrate was declared impeachable for "malpractice or neglect of duty." His salary was placed beyond legislative control. The council of revision idea was given up, the purely executive veto being substituted. The executive duties were declared to be to execute the laws and to make appointments not otherwise vested by the Constitution, the exception including judges, which were to be made, despite Wilson's apposition, by the upper house in accordance with Madison's motion.[35]

---

[32] The fact that Gerry asked Wilson whether he intended to have a council or not is a good illustration of the latter's leadership at this stage of the proceedings.

[33] This opposition was doubtless due to a belief that the small States would have a chance to participate in the personnel of a plural executive as much as to a jealousy of the executive.

[34] Pennsylvania and Maryland were the dissenters. The printed journal gives New York as divided. The Maryland vote was determined by a belief that the small States stood a better chance in an electoral college than in the legislature. This is purely inferential, but at a later time the other small States saw the matter in the same light.

[35] For the text of the amended resolutions, see Farrand, Records, vol. i, p. 235. The executive provisions are included in resolutions nos. 9 and 10, judicial provisions in no. 11.

This abandonment of the council type of executive was of the greatest importance. Every State but New York, as has been seen, possessed a separate council which formed a part of the magistracy. The council was likewise a familiar part of colonial government, and was emphasized in British constitutional theory. To take the step then taken demonstrated a willingness to break with the past that is explicable only in the light of the events which we have observed. The principle that executive efficiency and executive responsibility varied in inverse proportion to the size of the executive body had been so strongly inculcated and in so many different ways that it was strong enough to force the acceptance of a new principle of executive organization. Hitherto, as Mason of Virginia lamented at the close of the Convention's work, even "the Grand Signor himself had his Divan." [36]

Also it was true that, if the Convention was not ready to accept Wilson's principles of organization, they were equally unwilling to accept the opposing view of complete subordination of the executive and its complement, the unchecked legislature. The latter concept was placed before the Convention with sufficient clarity. Thus Madison reports:

Mr. Sherman said he considered the Executive magistracy as nothing more than an institution for carrying the will of the legislature into effect, that the person or persons ought to be appointed by and accountable to the Legislature only, which was the depository of the supreme will of the Society. They were the best judges of the business which ought to be done by the Executive department, and consequently of the number necessary from time to time for doing it, he wished the number might not be fixed, but that the legislature should be at liberty to appoint one or more as experience might dictate.[37]

He likewise "contended that the national Legislature should have power to remove the Executive at pleasure." [38] Bedford went even further, and "was opposed to every check on the Legislative, even the Council of Revision first proposed. He thought it would be sufficient to mark out in the

[36] Farrand, Records, vol. ii, p. 541.
[37] Ibid., vol. i, p. 65, note 1.
[38] Ibid., vol. i, p. 85.

Constitution the boundaries to the Legislative Authority, which would give all the requisite security to the rights of the other departments. The Representatives of the People were the best judges of what was for their interest, and ought to be under no external control whatever." [39]

The victory of the unit executive and qualified veto principles was thus an express repudiation of the principle of subordination in its extreme form. The status of the definition of executive powers and of the mode of election at the conclusion of the committee of the whole stage left the executive weak and dependent. But it was a real gain for the strong executives to secure a decisive defeat of the opposing principle.

It should be noted further that the close connection of centralization of power and the executive problem was not allowed to pass without notice. The speaker was Dickinson. Reverting to the familiar argument that a " firm Executive could only exist in a limited monarchy," he emphasized "the division of the Country into distinct States " as a "principal source of stability." [40] This was a timely reminder to those who were seeking consolidation that, even in a truly national State, the States were valuable agencies in making and enforcing the law. The matter was in reality totally distinct from the question of state sovereignty, however much it might have been confused with the latter at the time. Dickinson's was an appeal to the principles of local self-government against that of centralization, with its inevitable concomitant, a bureaucracy. This was necessary enough, when even Madison, who was never an extremist, was doubtful concerning the possibility of laying down any except very general limits on national competence. [41]

The completion of the work of the committee of the whole on the Virginia plan marked the beginning of the critical stage of the Convention's proceedings, opening with the sub-

---

[39] Ibid., vol. i, pp. 100–101.
[40] Ibid., vol. i, p. 86.
[41] Ibid., vol. i, p. 53.

mission of the Paterson plan, and renewed immediately as soon as the Convention reached those portions of the Committee's report which dealt with representation. Representation was continuously the great issue, and consequently questions relating to the executive were completely overshadowed.

The executive provisions of the Paterson plan are, however, not without interest, though perhaps framed as much with a view to win support from the Randolph-Mason type of large state delegates as to establish an executive regarded as intrinsically good. The characteristic features were the provision that the executive should be an organ completely distinct from the legislature, the retention of the plural executive, whose members were to be chosen by the legislature and not to be eligible for reëlection, and the remarkable provision, fathered by Dickinson,[42] that the executive should be removable by the legislature on application of a majority of state executives. The executive powers were defined as a "general authority to execute the federal acts," the appointment of all federal officers not otherwise provided for by the Constitution, including judges, and the direction of all military operations, without the power of personal command.[43] Since the government would operate to a great degree on the States rather than on individuals, the executive was empowered to call out the national forces for the purpose of coercing a recalcitrant member,[44] a provision in itself sufficient to discredit the whole plan.

Thus even the small States, when fighting for influence with the weapon of state sovereignty and weak government, accepted the principle of personal separation and that of executive control of military operations and of appointments. Indeed, with the exception of the omission of the veto provision, a very vital matter, however, there is a general similarity to the Virginia plan as originally submitted. Personal separation, executive appointment of officers, and executive

---

[42] Ibid., vol. i, p. 85.
[43] Ibid., vol. i, p. 244.
[44] Ibid., vol. i, p. 240.

control of the military may consequently be considered as accepted by all as correct principles, whatever differences might exist as to other matters. The lessons of state and national experience on these points had been too deeply impressed on the delegates' consciousness to permit their subordination even to influences with a more direct selfish appeal.

The submission of the Paterson resolutions had one indirect effect which certainly was not foreseen by their sponsors, namely, the famous speech by Hamilton in which he advocated a strengthening of the Virginia resolutions rather than a weakening of them, and submitted his sketch of a constitution, embodying his fundamental constitutional ideas.[45]

Inasmuch as Hamilton entered into no detailed analysis of his proposals, considerable caution must be observed in declaring what were his real intentions, but recommendations proceeding from such an important source can not be disregarded.

The Governor, to adopt Hamilton's title, was, in this plan, to be chosen by electors, in the manner contemplated by Wilson, and was to hold office during good behavior. He was to possess an absolute veto, the "execution of all laws passed," the direction of military operations in time of war, the power to make treaties, "with the advice and approbation of the Senate," the power to make all appointments, including those of ambassadors, subject to the veto of the Senate, and the "sole appointment of the heads or chief officers of the departments of Finance, War and Foreign Affairs." Removal of the chief magistrate was to be for "mal- and corrupt practice," all impeachments being triable by a court composed of the chief justices of the respective States.[46]

---

[45] Madison's version, Farrand, Records, vol. i, pp. 282–293; Yates' version, ibid., vol. i, pp. 294–301; Hamilton's brief, ibid., vol. i, pp. 304–311.

[46] The executive provisions are included in Art. IV of his sketch, Farrand, Records, vol. i, p. 292. Compare Art. IV of his fuller plan, which was never submitted. Farrand, Records, vol. iii, pp. 622–625. The chief difference between the two is in the fact that in the second two electoral colleges were provided.

It is difficult to deduce precisely what Hamilton had in mind to accomplish by these provisions. The question hinges chiefly on his comprehension of ministerial government as then practiced in Great Britain. Hamilton knew that the British Commons could "make the monarch tremble at the prospect of an innovation," referring to the recent experience in Great Britain with Fox and the India bill.[47] He believed, too, that the secret of that executive leadership which has always been inherent in the British Crown, whoever may exercise its powers, was preserved in Great Britain only by the use of "influence," a euphuism for the prevailing corruption.[48] The exclusion of the Senate from participation in the naming of the department chiefs points to a realization that these offices stood in a special relation to the chief magistrate. This evidence, however, is not conclusive that Hamilton was thinking of government through the ministers, rather than the chief magistrate. And yet the position he assumed when secretary of the treasury strengthens the feasibility of the assumption that he had something of the kind in mind: not, to be sure, weak ministerial government of the French type, but ministerial government characterized preëminently by executive leadership in the formulation of policy, tempered by the necessity of securing adoption of this policy by the legislative houses.[49]

The alternative to this interpretation would seem to be that Hamilton wished to remove the executive from all control. His chief magistrate, certainly, would have been amenable

---

[47] Federalist Papers, No. 71 (Lodge ed.), p. 449.

[48] Farrand, Records, vol. i, p. 376.

[49] We have seen that Hamilton believed that the determination of military and financial policy at least was an executive function (see above, chap. iv, note 55), and also that in the later days of Congress a large degree of actual control over policy initiation passed to the heads of the departments. In the absence of a clear understanding of the possibilities of the power of dissolution and of cabinet control of the time of the House of Commons, Hamilton, as did most, found in the power of the Crown to influence the two houses through patronage the explanation of the leadership. It is not a far fetched conclusion, then, to believe that Hamilton desired to institute something similar to this in the United States.

neither to the people nor to the legislature. The impeachment process provided was distinctly judicial in character. It certainly was not intended as a control over executive policy, for Hamilton would never have admitted state participation if he had believed that it would be utilized for such a purpose. The check of the Senate on the treaty making and appointing powers are the only exceptions admitted, that body being the war declaring body as well. The reason for this was, in Hamilton's own words, because "one of the weak sides of Republics was there being liable to foreign influences and corruption." [50]   But Hamilton's Senate was to serve for life, was to represent the wealth and aristocracy of the country. Responsibility to it would be a very different kind of responsibility from what Wilson had in mind.

Thus, whatever the interpretation placed on these proposals, it is plain that there was at its basis an idea totally different from Wilson's concept of the national representative, responsible to the whole people and subject at short periods to popular judgment. It may well be doubted, indeed, whether Hamilton ever fully understood this concept. His attempt to make himself prime minister under Washington, even his independent negotiations with Adams's cabinet members, point in this direction. He failed to see the incompatibility between the concept of the active chief magistrate, completely responsible, but to the people, not the legislature, and the practice of independent ministerial activities which had as their basis special relations between the minister and the lower house; to comprehend that the executive leadership in policy formulation which he desired should come through the instrumentality of presidential recommendations, not of those of the heads of the departments. In any event, the executive of the Constitution is not traceable to Hamilton's recommendations. Even senatorial participation in appointment and foreign affairs came from a different source, as will be noted in the proper place.

[50] Farrand, Records, vol. i, p. 289.

After the defeat of the Paterson plan and prior to a resumption of the discussion of the issue of representation, that portion of the amended Virginia plan which provided that no member of the legislature should hold any other office, State or national, during his term of office or for one year thereafter, was taken up for discussion.[51]   It is only the matter of holding national office that has a bearing on the executive problem, but the debate on this issue is interesting from several points of view.

The possession by ministers of seats in the legislature is, of course, of the essence of ministerial government.   The unanimity with which the leaders of 1787 rejected the principle is well known, even Hamilton being in favor of a prohibition of possession of other offices during the active term of the legislator.[52]   This had been quite generally attributed to the influence of theorists, and especially of Montesquieu, as if the framers of the Constitution were content to accept a political abstraction on its own merits and then apply it blindly.   We have seen, however, that in national affairs personal separation was dictated primarily by the very practical desire to get good executive officers and, at the same time, to secure a much-needed functional distribution, while in the State the primary motive was to obtain an external check on the legislature which would help to keep the legislature within the limits set by the Constitution.   This debate reveals another important influence which worked towards the same end, namely, British corruption.

British commentators on the history of American governmental institutions have, more than once, taken occasion to call attention to the fact that American political philosophy in the latter part of the eighteenth century was dominated by the doctrine of original—and ineradicable—political sin.[53] It is a fair answer to say that, in arriving at this conclusion,

---

[51] The blank in the original Virginia plan had been filled by the committee of the whole with 'one' (Farrand, Records, vol. i, p. 217).

[52] Ibid., vol. i, p. 352.

[53] A recent example is Pollard, Evolution of Parliament, p. 254.

the Fathers followed the inductive method, a great portion of their observation being devoted to English examples. But there is more than this involved in the matter. The men who made the Constitution were not so blind as to fail to see the very plain fact that ministers sat in Parliament. The full significance of this fact was obscured to many of them, but not to the extent that they did not realize at least the practical effects which were entailed.

Thus in the present debate the English-born Pierce Butler "appealed to the example of G. B. where men got into Parlt. that they might get offices for themselves or their friends. This was the source of the corruption that ruined their Govt." [54] Mason, likewise, declared:

I admire many parts of the British constitution and government, but I detest their corruption. Why has the power of the crown so remarkably increased the last century? A stranger, by reading their laws, would suppose it considerably diminished; and yet by the sole power of appointing the increased officers of government, corruption pervades every town and village in the kingdom.[55]

And, again, on the ensuing day, Butler cited British example:

What was the conduct of George the second to support the pragmatic sanction? To some of the opposers he gave pensions—others offices, and some, to put them out of the house of commons, he made lords. The great Montesquieu says, it is unwise to entrust persons with power, which by being abused operates to the advantage of those entrusted with it.[56]

And yet, on the other hand, Gorham and Hamilton at least were ready to defend, if not the process itself, at least the results of it.

" It was true," said the former, " abuses had been displayed in G. B. but no one cd. say how far they might have contributed to preserve the due influence of the Gov't nor what might have ensued in case the contrary theory had been tried." [57]

Hamilton " thought the remark of Mr. Ghorum a just one.

---

[54] Farrand, Records, vol. i, p. 376.
[55] Ibid., vol. i, p. 381.
[56] Ibid., vol. i, p. 391.
[57] Ibid., vol. i, p. 376.

It was impossible to say what wd. be the effect in G. B. of such a reform as had been urged. It was known that one of the ablest politicians, Mr. Hume, had pronounced all that influence on the side of the crown, which went under the name of corruption an essential part of the weight which maintained the equilibrium of the Constitution." [58]

A further conclusion that may thus be drawn is that these proponents of eligibility of legislators to office realized the value of the patronage which they proposed to vest in executive hands. They observed that it secured executive leadership in Great Britain; they knew that it had done the same thing in New York; they hoped to secure the same results in the national government. It is only by keeping this in mind that we can understand the full meaning of the debate on the provisions concerning appointment.

The debate on representation delayed any further consideration of the executive for almost a month, and it was not until the middle of July that the executive portions of the amended Virginia plan were resumed. But if these debates had no direct bearing on the executive questions, the final determination to which they led did. The small States, who held the balance of power between weak government and strong government adherents, had secured equality in one branch of the legislature. Their best efforts were henceforth to be directed towards an increase of senatorial power as over against the presidency, which was, since it was to be filled by the whole legislature, a large State office. Thus a new obstacle was placed in the way of the attainment by Wilson and his followers of their aim.

The executive resolutions proved a knotty problem, the sessions of almost an entire week being devoted to an attempt to establish the general principles of organization. The debate centered chiefly around the questions of method of elec-

---

[58] Ibid., vol. i, p. 376. Cf. Yates' version to Madison's, ibid., vol. i, p. 381. The vote on striking out the whole clause was four to four, three States divided. But this by no means indicated a desire to see legislators hold office while legislators.

tion, reëligibility and length of term. The weak executives felt that ineligibility was security enough for executive independence. Others claimed that the only way to avoid the undue dependence resulting from legislative election was tenure on good behavior. Small state influence and anti-democratic sentiment overwhelmed a renewal of Wilson's proposal for election by the people.[59] In all seven distinct methods of choice were suggested,[60] the final outcome being that the Convention reverted to the original plan, choice by the legislature, a seven-year term, and ineligibility.[61]

And yet, notwithstanding the failure of the independent executives to secure modification of the resolutions, they undoubtedly were gaining in strength, especially on the point of election by a source independent of the legislature. Able and influential leaders expressed their approbation of the idea. Gouverneur Morris, but recently returned from a long absence, warmly seconded his colleague's arguments for choice directly by the people, appealing, as had Wilson, to New York experience.[62] King, Paterson, Madison, Ellsworth and Gerry expressed approval of choice by electors at least.[63] Indeed, for a brief period the latter method was accepted, with only North and South Carolina and Georgia opposed.[64] Wilson could well declare that " he perceived with pleasure that the idea was gaining ground, of an election mediately or immediately by the people." [65]

The unqualified acceptance of the idea by Madison was doubtless the most important accession of strength. His early uncertainty was now gone and he declared decidedly:

It is essential . . . that the appointment of the Executive should either be drawn from some source, or held by some tenure, that will give him a free agency with regard to the Legislature. This could

[59] Nine States to one, Pennsylvania being affirmative.

[60] See Mason's speech, Farrand, Records, vol. ii, pp. 118–119.

[61] For the text of the executive resolutions submitted to the committee of detail, see ibid., vol. ii, p. 134.

[62] Ibid., vol. ii, p. 29. He also mentioned Connecticut.

[63] Ibid., vol. ii, pp. 56–58.

[64] Ibid., vol. ii, p. 58.

[65] Ibid., vol. ii, p. 56.

not be if he was to be appointed from time to time by the Legislature. It was not clear that an appointment in the 1st instance, even with an ineligibility afterwards, would not establish an improper connection between the two departments. Certain it was that the appointment would be attended with intrigues and contentions that ought not to be unnecessarily admitted. He was disposed for these reasons to refer the appointment to some other Source. The people at large was in itself the fittest. It would be as likely as any that could be devised to produce an Executive Magistrate of distinguished Character. . . . There was one difficulty however of a serious nature. . . . The right of suffrage was much more diffusive in the Northern than the Southern States. . . . The substitution of electors obviated this difficulty and seemed on the whole to be liable to the fewest objections.[66]

Gouverneur Morris was, however, the real floor leader[67] of those attached to the idea of the independent executive. His speeches of July 19[68] and July 24[69] were, it is evident from Madison's notes, masterly analyses of the whole question. Starting from the familiar " maxim in political Science that Republican Government is not adopted to a large extent of Country, because the energy of the Executive Magistracy can not reach the extreme parts of it," he declared Union impossible without an executive " provided with sufficient vigor to pervade every part of it."

" One great object of the Executive is to control the Legislature," he continued. It must "be the guardian of the people, even of the lower classes, ags. Legislative tyranny," the tyranny of the " Great and the wealthy who in the course of things will necessarily compose the Legislative body."

" Of all possible modes of appointment," he said in his second speech, "that by the Legislature is the worst." And then, with a comprehension of the British system remarkable for his day, he pointed to the possible evils of ministerial government:

In all public bodies there are two parties. The Executive will necessarily be more connected with one than the other. There will be a personal interest therefore in one of the parties to oppose as well as in the other to support him. Much had been said of the in-

---

[66] Ibid., vol. ii, pp. 56–57.
[67] The expression is used in an entirely figurative sense.
[68] Ibid., vol. ii, p. 52 ff.
[69] Ibid., vol. ii, pp. 103–105.

trigues that will be practiced by the Executive to get into office. Nothing had been said on the other side of the intrigues to get him out of office. Some leader or party will always covet his seat, will perplex his administration, will cabal with the Legislature, till he succeeds in supplanting him. This was the way in which the King of England was got out, he meant the real King, the Minister. This was the way in which Pitt (Ld. Chatham) forced himself into place. Fox was for pushing the matter still further. If he had carried his India bill, which he was very near doing, he would have made the Minister the King in form, almost as well as in substance. Our President will be the British Minister, yet we are about to make him appointable by the Legislature.

Under the influence of cogent arguments such as these, it was only natural that the cause they advocated should gain in popularity. The secret of its ultimate success was that it had in its support easily the leading minds of the Convention—Madison, Wilson, Gouverneur Morris, and Hamilton.

But Morris's remarks have an even greater interest than to demonstrate this ability of the leaders of the movement. They show a keen realization of the possible results of ministerial government—instability, legislative intrigue, and executive weakness. That their author did not see other possibilities, for example, that the ministry by controlling the time and the life of Parliament, and aided by party discipline, could be chosen by the latter and a part of it and still remain independent of it, may be forgiven him. Many English commentators have not yet realized it. And, after all, he might well answer, if reproached, that the British have but converted their Parliament into an electoral college for naming their real King, who remains independent of them. This was only what he advocated.[70]

Morris's comprehension of the essential difference between the executive that he was striving for and the British kingship received further illustration from a not unnatural error into which he fell, namely, of attempting to make the American chief magistrate unimpeachable, and his subsequent change of position.

[70] It is hardly necessary to say that this interpretation of British ministerial government is based on Sir Sidney Low's Governance of England.

He first argued:

> As to the danger from an unimpeachable magistrate, he could not regard it as formidable. There must be certain great officers of State; a minister of finance, of war, of foreign affairs etc. These he presumes will exercise their functions in subordination to the Executive, and will be amenable by impeachment to the public Justice, without these ministers the Executive can do nothing of consequence.[71]

But the error was of short duration. Morris's clear mind quickly perceived it, and he cried *peccavi:*

> Mr. Govr. Morris's opinion had been changed by the arguments used in the discussion. He was now sensible of the necessity of impeachments, if the Executive was to continue for any time in office. Our Executive was not like a Magistrate having a life interest, much less like one having an hereditary interest in his office. He may be bribed by a greater interest to betray his trust. . . . The Executive ought therefore to be impeachable for treachery; Corrupting his electors, and incapacity were other causes for impeachments. . . . This Magistrate is not the King, but the prime-minister. The people are the King.[72]

In that happy phrase, "the magistrate is not the King, but the prime-minister; the people are the King," Morris aptly expressed the idea for which he and Wilson and Madison were working. Political powers were the people's. The royal prerogative was in them. Irresponsibility attached to them alone. The chief magistrate would be their servant, as in theory the prime minister was the King's, and would owe his responsibility to them. The prerogative, being no longer something separate and apart from the people, there was no need for an indirect responsibility through ministers and the popular house to the people. It should be to the people direct. This was the concept which was steadily gaining ground.

Objection may be raised to this interpretation that the independent executive was growing in favor on the ground that its advocates were unable to hold the temporary gain that they made in securing the acceptance of the electoral college idea. The answer to this lies in the fact that with the small

[71] Farrand, Records, vol. ii, pp. 53–54.
[72] Ibid., vol. ii, p. 69.

States the question of representation outweighed in importance any other consideration. It was on the rock of apportionment of electors that the tentative scheme was wrecked.

The vote by which the provision was first adopted was taken on the first clause of a motion by Ellsworth to strike out choice by the legislature and to substitute choice by electors, apportioned in the proportion of one for each State not exceeding 200,000 in population,[73] two for each State between 200,000 and 300,000 and three for each State exceeding 300,000. Electors were to be chosen by the state legislatures.[74]

This would have been a great gain for the small States, for as Madison pointed out, almost all of them could look forward to the day when they would have three electors, so "that this ratio ought either to be made temporary, or so varied as that it would adjust itself to the growing population of the States." [75]

Consequently, Gerry moved as a substitute for the permanent plan proposed by Ellsworth that "*in the first instance*" electors be allotted on a fixed basis, which was adopted.[76] The trend of this motion was indicated by Williamson's motion that the number of electors be regulated by their representation in the lower House.[77] However, before an attempt was made to establish a permanent basis, the Convention reverted to choice by the legislature.

The reason for this is now apparent enough. The small States were willing to accept the principle of the independent representative executive, if properly recompensed. When, as by Ellsworth's resolution, they were satisfied on the score of

---

[73] The printed journal gives 100,000.

[74] Ibid., vol. ii, p. 57. Previously a motion by Martin for choice of electors chosen by the State legislature had secured the consent of only Maryland and Delaware. Vol. ii, p. 32. It was in this fashion that the entering wedge for equality in the Senate had been inserted, for this method meant at least one electoral vote for each State. The move for the electoral college was thus at this stage initiated by the small States.

[75] Ibid., vol. ii, p. 63.

[76] Ibid., vol. ii, p. 63. The italics are Madison's.

[77] Ibid., vol. ii, p. 64.

representation, they were willing to join with the two large States in which a majority were for the independent executive. This resulted in the vote of July 19, Connecticut, New Jersey, Delaware, and Maryland joining Virginia and Pennsylvania in favor of the electoral scheme as then organized against the three southernmost States, with Massachusetts divided.[78]

Madison's remarks, Gerry's motion and Williamson's suggestion, however, combined to show the small States that the large ones were not yet ready to pay their price. But alone they were unable to withstand a combination of those large States which opposed the whole idea of non-legislative choice with Virginia and Pennsylvania, Gerry's motion being carried six to four, the small States making the minority.

Consequently, when the matter was reconsidered, New Jersey and Delaware, together with New Hampshire, whose delegates had just arrived, joined the three southernmost States and Massachusetts to restore the original method.[79]

As Pinckney had said in the debate on representation in the legislature, the whole matter came to this: if the small States got what they wanted in the way of representation, they were, in general, for a "high-toned" government, but, holding the balance of power, they intended to use it. Connecticut and Maryland were willing even to accept the independent executive without a guarantee as to representation. The objection to the principle of the representative executive was thus confined to North and South Carolina and Georgia and to minorities elsewhere, for Massachusetts could be expected at least to divide her vote on a clear-cut issue. If the strong executive forces were able to avail themselves of their opportunities for a bargain, their situation was far less hopeless than it appeared.

The truth is that, while the Convention thought itself ready

---

[78] Ibid., vol. ii, p. 58. Ghoram and Strong must have cast the negative Massachusetts votes, as King and Gerry had expressed themselves in favor of the idea.

[79] Farrand, Records, vol. ii, p. 101.

to proceed to the business of drawing up a draft of a constitution on the basis of the general principles, so far as the executive was concerned they had settled practically nothing except the question of unity and the veto power. The time which they believed they had devoted to establishment of the general principles of executive organization had, in fact, but served to prepare the way for the adoption of other principles. That this was true was due to the devoted efforts of a small group of active proponents of executive independence and strength, at whose head stood Wilson and Morris, and their convert, Madison. By forwarding their plan at every juncture that afforded a possibility, they were making possible a final settlement in which they would gain much of what they desired.

CHAPTER V

THE PRESIDENCY IN THE FEDERAL CONVENTION: LATER PHASES

On July 23, when the Convention had concluded its consideration of all save the executive propositions of the report of the committee of the whole, it was moved by Gerry, and unanimously resolved by the Convention, "that the proceedings of the Convention for the establishment of a National Government (except the part relating to the Executive), be referred to a Committee to prepare and report a Constitution conformable thereto."[1] Having fixed the number of its membership at five, on the succeeding day the Convention chose as members Rutledge, Randolph, Gorham, Ellsworth and Wilson.[2] After two days of further debate on the executive resolutions, they were referred, and with them the Paterson resolutions and the plan which in the early days of the Convention Charles Pinckney had submitted.

The general language of the Convention's mandate to this committee of detail, as it was called, afforded it ample opportunity to play an influential part in determining the final character of the Constitution. It could, to be sure, neither change any of the principles already adopted nor introduce new ones palpably not in harmony with them. But it displayed no hesitancy in interpreting its mandate as justifying an expansion of the amended resolutions, especially in the direction of a more complete definition of powers, by additions to which the Convention had given no prior sanction.

This matter of definition of powers was a vital one to the executive department. The only powers explicitly conferred on the executive thus far were the veto power, the power to make appointments, though not of judges, and a power,

---

[1] Farrand, Records, vol. ii, p. 95.
[2] Ibid., vol. ii, p. 106.

which perhaps was only a duty, to execute the laws. We
have seen that Madison's original idea had been to leave the
unenumerated powers to the will of the legislature as expressed through legislative enactments.   Patently it was
vastly important whether the committee would adopt this
plan or another.   Should the great political powers, such as
control of the military, control of foreign negotiations, the
power of pardon, be left to the will of future legislatures,
or be fixed by the Constitution beyond legislative control?
Even more fundamental was the question of the vesting
clause.   Should executive power be possessed by the chief
executive subject to the law of the land, or on the same footing as the legislature possessed its powers?   Again, should
a complete enumeration of powers be undertaken?   If not,
should the unenumerated power be left to the legislature to
grant or withhold?   State constitutions furnished examples
of each method of procedure.   The nature of the committee's
action, whether as to the quantum of executive power or the
terms on which the chief magistrate should possess it, might
well change the whole character of the national executive.
A careful consideration of its personnel, its procedure and its
work seems consequently well justified.

The personnel seems to have been determined primarily by
a desire to represent the different sections of the country.
Thus there were two representatives from the South, two
from the East and one from the Central States.   The small
States, however, did not fare so well, for not only did they
have but a single representative, but the member chosen,
Ellsworth, was by no means an extreme particularist, he and
his colleague Johnson having cast Connecticut's vote against
the Paterson plan over Sherman's opposition.[3]   Choice of
individuals was determined primarily by legal ability or, in
the case of Gorham, political prominence.   Except for
Gorham, the members were lawyers of note.   The membership includes a chief justice of the supreme bench, a nominee

---

[3] Sherman's position was fairly extreme, and, since there were
only three delegates, the conclusion seems correct.

to the same office, whose appointment was defeated for political reasons, a justice of the same court and an attorney-general. Ellsworth's abilities are further attested by his authorship of the judiciary act.

On the question of executive power and organization, the committee was almost equally divided. Of Wilson's position we have already given sufficient indication. As to the others, Rutledge and Randolph were certainly favorable to a weak executive. While the former had approved executive unity, he had opposed appointment of the judiciary by the executive and had vigorously upheld election by the legislature, with ineligibility, as preferable to choice by an independent source.[4] Randolph had gone a step further and inveighed bitterly against the unit executive as the " foetus of monarchy."[5] Gorham's position can not be stated with so much certainty. He had voted for a term of seven years when the executive was to be chosen by the legislature and ineligible for reëlection, and had supported appointment of the judges by the executive, giving expression on that occasion to a marked distrust of legislative assemblies. He had moved to strike out ineligibility of members of Congress to public office, expressing a belief that the Crown's influence in Great Britain was an element of constitutional strength. On the other hand, he must have supported election of the chief magistrate by the legislature, as has been pointed out. Certainly, then, he can not be classed as a partisan of an out and out strong executive. Perhaps it is correct to say merely that he had tendencies in that direction.[6] Ellsworth undoubtedly believed in the principle of a strong, independent executive, as he was later to demonstrate in the debates in the Senate on the question of removal of department heads. Connecticut's vote,

---

[4] Farrand, Records, vol. i, pp. 65, 119; vol. ii, p. 57.

[5] Ibid., vol. i, p. 66; vol. ii, pp. 43, 54.

[6] For Ghoram's positions on these points see Farrand, Records, vol. i, pp. 72, 381; vol. ii, pp. 42, 58 and above, chap. iv, note 71. An attempt has been made to connect Ghoram with von Steuben's negotiations with Prince Henry of Prussia, but the evidence is very slight. Richard Krauel, Prince Henry of Prussia and the Regency of the United States, in American Historical Review, vol. xvii, p. 44.

and hence Ellsworth's, for Sherman certainly voted no, had been cast for executive unity. He had sought to create an electoral college which would satisfy small state aspirations, and, when some of the small States reverted to the original scheme, had, with Johnson, maintained Connecticut in its support of the electoral college principle. However, he was the representative of a small State, and, as such, had favored senatorial choice of the judiciary after the equal vote determination. On the whole, therefore, the statement that there was a fairly even balance seems justified, but with this qualification. In so far as Ellsworth's small state interests overcame his belief in executive strength, just that far would the influence of a majority of the committee be favorable to enhancement of senatorial, at the expense of presidential, power. This was a significant fact.[7]

The executive provisions of the amended Virginia plan, of course, formed the basis of the committee's work. Of the other two documents before them, the Paterson resolutions could be of little value, but the same is not true of the Pinckney plan.

Thanks to the researches of Professors Jameson and Mc-Loughlin, the student of today can speak with a degree of certainty concerning this document which for so long proved a mystery. An outline of the plan and an excerpt from its provisions, fortunately for our purposes that portion concerning the executive powers, have been discovered in the papers of James Wilson and completely identified. By comparing with these Pinckney's pamphlet published just after the Convention's adjournment,[8] the executive of Pinckney's plan may be reproduced with considerable fullness.

The Wilson outline, articles five and six, reads as follows:

The Senate and H. D. [House of Delegates] shall by joint ballot

---

[7] There is no evidence that the committee balloted on any point, but the balance of opinion is none the less worthy of note.

[8] Observations on the Plan of Government Submitted to the Federal Convention. Farrand, Records, vol. iii, p. 106 ff. For the most complete and authoritative restoration of the Pinckney plan, see Farrand, Records, vol. iii, appendix D.

annually chuse the Presidt. U.-S. from among themselves or the
People at large.—In the Presidt. the executive Authority of the U.
S. shall be vested.—His Powers and Duties—He shall have a Right
to advise with the Heads of the different Departments as his Council.
Council of Revision, consisting of the Presidt. S. for for. Affairs,
S. of War, Heads of the Departments of Treasury and Admiralty
or any two of them togr wt the Presidt.[9]

The definition of powers contained in Wilson's excerpt can
also best be given in full:

There shall be a President, in which the Ex. Authority of the U.
S. shall be vested. It shall be his Duty to inform the Legislature of
the Condition of U. S. so far as may respect his Department—to
recommend matters to their Consideration—to correspond with the
Executives of the several States—to attend to the Execution of the
Laws of the U. S.—to transact Affairs with the Officers of Government, civil and military—to expedite all such Measures as may be resolved on by the Legislature—inspect the Departments of foreign
Affairs—War—Treasury—Admiralty—to reside where the Legislature shall sit—to commission all Officers, and keep the Great Seal
of U. S.—He shall, by Virtue of his Office, be Commander in chief
of the Land Forces of U. S. and Admiral of their Navy—He shall
have power to convene the legislature on extraordinary occasions—
to prorogue them, provided such Prorogation shall not exceed
Days in the space of any —He may suspend officers, civil and military.[10]

In his "Observations," Pinckney sheds additional light
concerning his intentions. To the duty "to attend to the
Execution of the Laws of the U. S." he adds the phrase "by
the several States," evidently intending by the clause something of the kind suggested by Paterson, rather than a general law enforcement and administrative power, which, as
has been seen above, was amply provided for by other clauses.
The President himself was to be an administrative officer,
being "charged with all the business of the Home Department." The presidential power to inspect the departments
would "operate," the pamphlet declares, "as a check upon
those officers, keep them attentive to their duty, and may be
the means in time not only of preventing and correcting
errors, but of detecting and punishing mal-practices." Also

[9] Ibid., vol. ii, p. 135. Annual was a mistake for septennial. See
ibid., vol. i, 68; vol. iii, p. 110. His executive was to be eligible
for reëlection, according to the "Observations."
[10] Ibid., vol. ii, p. 158.

the President might "consider the principals of the Departments as his Council, and . . . acquire their advice and assistance, whenever the duties of his Office shall render it necessary. By this means our Government will possess what it has always wanted, but never yet had, a Cabinet Council. An institution essential in all Governments, whose situation or connections oblige them to have an intercourse with other powers." The recommending function is expanded into the duty "to prepare and digest, in concert with the great departments, such business as will come before the Legislature, at their stated sessions." The power of appointment was to be possessed by the President, with the exception of judicial and diplomatic officers.[11]

Without at this point entering into a discussion of the influence of this. plan on the committee's report, it is due Pinckney to say that, as an abstract question, his concept of what constituted executive power was remarkably complete, and his treatment of it far more satisfactory than that of the Virginia plan. The existence of the Wilson excerpt is not accidental. It was made because of the fact that Pinckney had afforded by far the most complete enumeration of executive powers submitted at any time to the Convention's attention, and one characterized by careful and original thought on the subject.

The origin of much of it is very plainly the New York constitution, a further evidence of the interest which the New York executive provisions had aroused in students of government. Those clauses which concerned the general possession of executive power, that is, the general vesting clause, military control, convening and proroguing the legislature, the sessional message of information, the right to make recommendations, and what may be called the law enforcement clauses, were all taken almost verbatim from that instrument. Exactly as Wilson, in searching for an accurate description of executive power, turned to Pinckney's draft,

---

[11] Ibid., vol. iii, p. 111.

so Pinckney had turned to the powers exercised by Governor Clinton.[12]

With these materials at its disposal, the committee began its work by assigning to Governor Randolph, as the mover of the original resolutions, the honor of making the first draft of the Constitution proper.[13] This draft was submitted to the committee for discussion and emendation.[14] The amended draft was then entrusted to Wilson for further expansion. The Wilson draft, after further amendment by the committee, became the report of the committee.[15]

Thanks to the labors of modern investigators, and equally to Professor Farrand's monumental work, it will be possible to trace this expansion of the meager provisions of the Virginia resolutions into the enumeration of powers of Article II of the Constitution with accuracy, a matter of the greater

---

[12] The relevant portions of the New York Constitution are given for purposes of comparison: "The supreme executive power and authority of this State shall be vested in a governor." Art. xvii. "He shall, by virtue of his office, be general and commander-in-chief of all the militia, and admiral of this state; he shall have power to convene the assembly and senate on extraordinary occasions; to prorogue them from time to time, provided such prorogation shall not exceed sixty days in the space of any one year." Art. xviii. "It shall be the duty of the governor to inform the legislature at every session of the condition of the state so far as may concern his department; to recommend such matters to their consideration as shall appear to him to concern its good government, welfare, and prosperity; to correspond with the Continental Congress and other States; to transact all necessary business with the officers of government, civil and military; to take care that the laws are faithfully executed to the best of his ability; and to expedite all such matters as may be resolved upon by the legislature." Art. xix. The council of revision provision is of course but a modification of the New York idea.

[13] A facsimile of this document is published in Meigs, Growth of the Constitution, following p. 316. It has all the ear marks of a first draft, especially the introductory statement of the general principles on which a constitution should be drafted. Farrand, Records, vol. ii, pp. 137–150.

[14] This is a reasonable inference from the fact that each clause is checked off, and that amendments are written into it by Rutledge, the chairman. That Rutledge was chairman is shown by the fact that his name stands first in the list of members and also he made the committee's report. Farrand, Records, vol. ii, pp. 97, 106, 176, 190.

[15] The emendations are again in Rutledge's hand. For text, with emendations, see ibid., vol. ii, pp. 163–175.

importance as the enumeration then made was not subsequently changed by the Convention.   In fact, it is possible to do even more than this, for among Wilson's papers have been discovered documents which illustrate the different stages of his work : the first consisting of a preamble, a part of a legislative article, and an outline of the remainder ; the second, which is incomplete, a first draft, from which the executive article is missing, but which contained, pinned within it, the excerpt of the Pinckney plan ; the third, the final draft submitted for the committee's approval.[16]

Since the committee was not at liberty to vary the principles of organization, the interest in this process centers chiefly on the question of powers.   How far would the committee go in adding other functions to those which the Convention had already sanctioned ?

Randolph was evidently not willing to go far.   His draft read :

His powers shall be : 1. to carry into execution the national laws ; 2. to command and superintend the militia, 3. to direct their discipline, 4. to direct the executives of the states to call them or any part for the support of the national government, 5. to appoint to offices not otherwise provided for, 6. to be removeable on impeachment, made by the house of representatives and conviction of malpractice or neglect of duty, before the supreme judiciary, 7. to receive a fixed compensation for the devotion of his time to the public service the quantum of which shall be settled by the national legislature to be paid out of the national treasury, 8. to have a qualified negative on legislative acts so as to require repassing by 2/3. 9. and shall swear fidelity to the union, as the legislature shall direct. 10. receiving ambassadors. 11. commissioning officers. 12. convene legislature.[17]

---

[16] These identifications are Professor Farrand's. For the text of these documents respectively, see ibid., vol. ii, pp. 150–151, 152–163, 163–175. The text of the final report is given in vol. ii, pp. 177–189.

[17] W. M. Meigs, Growth of the Constitution, facsimile, sheets vi and vii. Farrand, Records, vol. ii, pp. 145–146. Certain portions of this enumeration are deleted in the draft as it stands today. Professor Farrand prints these deletions as made by Randolph himself. It seems more reasonable to infer that where the deletions occur in connection with emendations by Rutledge that they were the results of committee action. This hypothesis is supported by the fact that the amendments are incorporated into Wilson's draft, proving that they had the whole committee's sanction. Some of the deletions

It will be noted that only a single function connected with foreign affairs was assigned the chief executive, the power to receive ambassadors.   With the rest Randolph dealt in what must have seemed to the strong executive supporters a very cavalier fashion.   Originally, in enumerating the legislative powers, he had included the power " to make treaties of commerce under the foregoing restrictions.   To make treaties of peace or alliance under the foregoing restrictions, and without the surrender of territory for an equivalent, and, in no case unless a superior title."   In the margin opposite each he noted " qu. as to senate."   Further in the list he included the power " to send ambassadors." [18]   In the final draft, these provisions are crossed out, and at the end of the legislative article it is declared in Randolph's hand that " the powers destined for the senate peculiarly are 1. To make treaties of commerce 2. to make peace 3. to appoint the judiciary." [19] It may be that the original treaty-making clauses inserted in the description of legislative powers were deleted by Randolph himself, the explanation being that before he finished his article he decided to vest these powers in the Senate.   It is quite probable, however, that he retained both clauses, the query as to the Senate simply indicating that the sole control of the Senate was an open matter.   In either case, it is plain that Randolph regarded foreign affairs as a matter to be decided either by the legislature as a whole or by the Senate. If the latter body were to make treaties, and the legislature as a whole to send ambassadors, the executive power to receive ambassadors must have proved, as it was doubtless meant to, purely a formal one.

This article of Randolph's was of the more importance as up until this time the Convention had, so far as the records

were made with a careless vigor far more characteristic of Rutledge's chirography than of Randolph's careful neatness.

[18] W. M. Meigs, Growth of the Constitution, facsimile, sheet v; Farrand, Records, vol. ii, p. 143.   The " foregoing restrictions " had to do with the number of votes required for passing a navigation act. It is not clear just what Randolph meant.

[19] W. M. Meigs, Growth of the Constitution, facsimile, sheet vi; Farrand, Records, vol. ii, p. 145.

show, given the subject of control of foreign affairs no attention at all, the sole recorded reference to it being that in the
provisions of Hamilton's sketch whereby treaties should be
made and ambassadors named by the executive with the
advice and consent of the Senate.[20]   That Randolph should
have given the topic the treatment he did is not to be won-
dered at in view of his weak executive proclivities, already
commented on.   He had, indeed, previously declared it to be
his opinion that the Senate might sit constantly, "perhaps to
aid the executive." [21]

If the Rutledge emendations be accepted as the result of
committee action, it may be said that the other members
showed a tendency to correct the more manifest executive
weaknesses inherent in Randolph's language.   Thus, where
Randolph provided only for executive control of a militia the
calling of which into service was to be dependent on the state
executives, the committee gave the much more far-reaching
power "to be Commander in Chief of the Land & Naval
Power of the Union & of the Militia of the sevl. States."
Other amendments added the power to "propose to the
Legisle. from Time to Time by Speech or Mess such Meas
as concern this Union," and, inferentially, the pardon power,
which was declared not pleadable to an impeachment, substituted "Treason, Bribery or Corruption" for Randolph's
more general definition of grounds for impeachment, placed
the executive's salary and the question of his fidelity to the
Union beyond legislative control, and limited the exceptions
to the executive appointing power to those enumerated in the
fundamental law.[22]

With respect to the special senatorial powers, however, the
changes made were in the direction of making the upper
house the sole organ for controlling foreign affairs.   The
power to send ambassadors was transferred from the general

[20] Farrand, Records, vol. i, p. 292.
[21] Ibid., vol. i, p. 415.
[22] W. M. Meigs, Growth of the Constitution, facsimile, sheet vi;
Farrand, Records, vol. ii, p. 145.

legislative to the special senatorial category, and in addition Randolph's second clause was made to read, " to make treaties of peace and alliance." Also the restrictions on the treaty-making power, which Randolph had originally included, disappeared.

On a still more important point concessions were made to the small state interest. The legislature was, of course, to choose the executive. But was it to be by joint ballot or by the two houses separately? More hinged on the decision than appears on the surface. To the small state delegates influence in election, we have seen, was the controlling factor. A joint ballot would give them little advantage. A separate ballot would make them tenacious of legislative choice.

Randolph's draft had dodged the issue by providing merely that " the executive 1. shall consist of a single person, 2. who shall be elected by the Legislature." Rutledge's first emendation had been " by joint Ballot." But later " joint" was stricken out, and the whole clause made to read " who shall be elected by the Legislature by ballot each Ho, havg. a Negative on the other." [23]   Through Ellsworth's influence, we may imagine, small State demands were thus completely satisfied.

With the amended Randolph draft as the basis of his work, Wilson now proceeded to draft the committee's report. To a far greater extent than Randolph, he was merely the draftsman. But nevertheless more significance attaches to his work than a merely textual one. The choice of language, especially as concerns the vesting clause, was a matter that, might have, and in fact did have, most momentous consequences. We have seen that state practice had varied widely, and that, as a general rule, forms of expression had been used which invited legislative interference. As might have been expected, Wilson fell into no such error. His draft of the excerpt from the Pinckney plan was for a purpose— namely, to utilize it, and through it the New York constitu-

---

[23] Ibid.

tion, as a model, so far as it was relevant, for the description of the national executive powers.

A comparison of the outline and the excerpt quoted above with the following quotation from the original final Wilson draft will demonstrate how greatly the latter was influenced by the former:

> The Executive Power of the United States shall be vested in a single person. His Title shall be "The President of the United States of America";[24] and his Title shall be "His Excellencey." ... He shall from Time to Time give information of the State of the Nation; he may recommend Matters to their Consideration, and he may convene them on extraordinary Occasions. He shall take Care to the best of his Ability that the laws be faithfully executed. He shall commission all the Officers in all Cases of the United States and shall appoint Officers in all Cases not otherwise provided for by this Constitution. He shall receive Ambassadors, and shall correspond with the Governors and other Executive Officers of the several States. He shall have power to grant Reprieves and Pardons, but his Pardon shall not be pleadable in Bar of an Impeachment. He shall be Commander in Chief of the Army and Navy of the United States, and of the Militia of the Several States.[25]

With unimportant verbal changes, this draft became the report of the Committee, and finally the constitutional enumeration of the executive powers. The executive which had gone into the committee with only the appointing power, the veto power, and the power to execute the laws, came out, not only with additional powers, but with all of them granted in terms which left no loophole for subsequent legislative interference. What have come to be known as the political powers were now the President's, and the President's alone, so far as the Constitution itself could settle the matter. The credit for the latter belongs jointly to Wilson and to Pinckney. It may well be believed that Wilson might have gone direct to the New York constitution for his phraseology. But the fact is that it was the Pinckney plan that he used in determining the phraseology of this part of the executive article.

---

[24] The style adopted by the Committee had been "Gouvernour of the United People & States of America." While of course the title was a familiar one, Pinckney and Wilson can be given the credit for its selection for the national chief magistrate.

[25] Farrand, Records, vol. ii, pp. 171–172.

Indeed, the inclusion of the important power of recommending measures to the legislature was, it is reasonable to believe, if not determined, certainly strongly suggested by the existence of the Pinckney draft.   Again it may be true that the power would have been included in any event, but the fact remains that the Rutledge amendment is but the substance of Pinckney's provision, and the language used by Wilson is that of his excerpt from Pinckney's draft.

It may, perhaps, be objected that Pinckney was, at best, only a copyist.   To this it may be answered that the willingness to carry over into the national government the powers of the strongest state executive is the point at issue, rather than a question of phraseology.   Pinckney was willing to do this, where Madison had been hesitant, had moved for a legislative definition of powers.   The result was that the committee had before it an extensive enumeration of executive powers which it indubitably used even to the extent of adopting the title provided.   This, it is believed, is sufficient warrant for attributing to Pinckney a very real influence on Article II of the finished Constitution.[26]

The greatest result of the committee's work was thus the inclusion of one main element of the Wilson executive plan— an independent possession by the executive department of its powers by direct grant of the people.   It remained to be seen whether the other cardinal feature, election by a source independent of the legislature, could be secured.

There is one phase of the question of Wilson's choice of a vesting clause that should be noted, though it can not be answered, namely, whether or not the enumerated powers were intended by him or the committee to be an exhaustive

---

[26] It should be observed that Pinckney had moved to strike out Madison's motion to permit the legislature to confer executive powers on the chief magistrate on the grounds that the power was included in the general power to execute the laws.   It is not a very far fetched inference to conclude that his motive may have been a dislike for this way of giving the executive powers.   On the other hand, it was Randolph who seconded him, and Randolph was hardly actuated by this motive.

description of that general executive power with which the President was endowed. On this point there is absolutely no evidence, so far as the writer can discover. Certainly some state constitutions had realized that there was a field of unenumerated powers and had made various arrangements concerning its exercise. On the other hand, the fact that exactly the same language was used concerning the other two departments militates against a conclusion that Wilson had any ulterior motive in view. Perhaps the point did not arise in his mind. Nevertheless the expression used certainly vested whatever of executive power might be inferred from any parts of the Constitution in the executive alone.

The loss by the executive of the power to control foreign affairs, hardly affected by a last-minute change of the senatorial power to send ambassadors for the paler power 'to appoint ambassadors,'[27] was a serious matter for those who desired to strengthen the President's hands. But it was by no means certain that the controlling coalition of small States and weak executive proponents which controlled the committee could be maintained in the Convention. Nor can the committee's action be interpreted as expressing the will of the parent body. It was the result of the constitution of the committee, which had been determined by very different factors than the attitude of the members on the matter of executive power.[28]

The history of the executive article during the period following the report of the committee of detail centers about two main points, the attempt of Gouverneur Morris and Charles Pinckney to create a cabinet council for the President, and incidentally to provide a complete organization

---

[27] The expression 'send' is in the amended Wilson draft, but not in the final printed report. Wilson had also declared simply that the Senate should have 'the power to make treaties,' discarding the descriptive phrases used by Randolph, a change continued in the printed report. Farrand, Records, vol. ii, pp. 169, 183.

[28] The decision of the committee to enumerate the legislative powers of the national government determined finally that the States would continue to perform the more important part of law making and hence law enforcing for the Union as a whole.

of the administrative departments, and the final settlement by a special committee of eleven of the problem of the choice of the chief magistrate and that of the executive powers of the Senate.

The first of these, so far as the Constitution is concerned, had, as is well known, only a single result, namely, the inclusion of that clause which permits the chief executive to require as he saw fit the advice of the heads of the departments in writing. The chief interest of the proposal lies thus not in what was accomplished, but rather in the light that is thrown by it on the question of the relation intended of the President to the administrative chiefs.

Such light is indeed welcome, for, prior to this time, direct evidence on the subject is sadly wanting. Indeed, this general failure of the Convention to devote any of its time to the matter of the President's relation to administration, coupled with the fact that the departments were only casually mentioned in the completed instrument, has very generally been interpreted to signify that this phase of executive power was not present in the minds of the Constitution makers.

In view of the very evident tendency in the national government under the Articles towards administrative integration, and especially in view of the desire manifested in Jefferson's proposals to relieve Congress of administrative work by inserting between it and the departments a responsible head of administration, the tenableness of this interpretation is shaken. It has been seen, too, that the original concept of executive power held by the Convention was that primarily of law enforcement. The insistence on this point of view may be reasonably interpreted as having reference to administrative laws as well as laws in the strict sense of the term. It is not an extravagant inference to conclude that a general oversight of the business of the administrative officers was, to a degree at least, involved in the general expression "execution of the laws," as well as the enforcement of the judicial decisions of the courts.

But direct evidence that this is true is slight. What there is points to this conclusion. It consists of only two facts— the proposal of Hamilton on June 18 that the chief magistrate "have the sole appointment of the heads or chief officers of the departments of Finance, War and Foreign Affairs" and only the nomination of other officers,[29] and Morris's statement that "there must be certain great officers of State; a minister of finance, of war, of foreign affairs, etc. These he presumes will exercise their functions in subordination to the Executive."[30] Certainly both of these men thought of the heads of departments, finance and all, as but subordinates of the President performing under his control functions which the President was unable to perform himself.

On the other hand, the original Pinckney plan provided for choice of the administrative heads by Congress,[31] while the President was himself to serve as a sort of secretary of the interior. The Pinckney council would have been much the same sort of organ as the state privy councils, both an administrative body and a ready means for legislative control of the President, whatever might have been Pinckney's intentions.

The incongruity of such a body with Wilson's plan has already been commented upon, as well as his success in preventing the adoption of any such scheme. Nevertheless the idea of some sort of council composed of heads of the departments early received informal consideration. Mason spoke of the suggestion "either within or without doors" of composing the council of revision in such a fashion.[32] At about the same time the French chargé wrote also of "un Président élu pour six années et son Conseil composé des differens Ministres d'États," who should together exercise the right of qualified veto.[33]

---

[29] Farrand, Records, vol. i, p. 292.
[30] Ibid., vol. ii, p. 52.
[31] Wilson outline, article xv; ibid., vol. ii, p. 136.
[32] Ibid., vol. i, p. 111.
[33] Otto to Montmorin, June 10, 1787; Farrand, Records, vol. iii, p. 40.

No formal action, however, was taken until on August 18 Ellsworth " observed that a Council had not yet been provided for the President " and suggested such a body to be composed of the Chief Justice, the President of the Senate and the ministers " who should advise but not conclude the President." Pinckney then requested that the proposition lie over as Gouverneur Morris had previously given like notice. This was done, although Gerry gave expression to his dislike to " letting the heads of the departments, particularly of finance, have anything to do in business connected with legislation," and Dickinson " urged that the great appointments should be made by the Legislature, in which case they might properly be consulted by the Executive—but not if made by the Executive himself." [34]

On August 20th the Morris-Pinckney plan was submitted. It provided for a complete constitutional organization of the executive department.   There were to be five departments, at the head of which, respectively, were to be a secretary of domestic affairs, of commerce and finance, of foreign affairs, of war, and of marine.   They, together with the Chief Justice, were to compose a Council of State " to assist the President in conducting the Public affairs," and for the purpose of furnishing advice, written if requested, on matters submitted to them by the President.   This advice was, however, not to conclude the President, who was to exercise his own judgment, though every department head was to be " responsible " for his opinion on the affairs relating to his particular department.

These ministers were to be appointed by the President alone and to hold their offices during pleasure.   They were also to be subject to impeachment and removal, " for neglect of duty, malversation, or corruption."   They were to possess a large proportion of that right of recommendation which was their natural heritage from their forbears under the Articles.   Especially significantly, the secretary of commerce

[34] Ibid., vol. ii, p. 329.

and finance was "to prepare and report plans of revenue and for the regulation of expenditures, and also to recommend such things as may in his Judgment promote the commercial interests of the U. S." [35]

Certainly this plan serves strongly to confirm the opinion that the chief magistrate was regarded, by its authors at least, as the active chief of administration. The department heads were certainly conceived as completely subordinate to the chief executive, since they were to be appointable by the President alone and to hold office at his pleasure. Nor is there any distinction made between departments on any basis of special relationship to the President. Inasmuch as control of foreign affairs at this stage was completely vested in the Senate, only the military departments could be said to have any special relation to an enumerated power.

The enumeration of the duties of these department heads will serve further to demonstrate the fact that the executive was envisaged in this plan as the head of administration. The secretary of domestic affairs was to "attend to matters of general police, the state of Agriculture and manufactures, the opening of roads and navigations, and the facilitating communications through the United States." The secretary of commerce and finance was "to superintend all matters relating to the public finances." The secretary of foreign affairs had for his functions "to correspond with all foreign Ministers, prepare plans of Treaties, and consider such as may be transmitted from abroad; and generally to attend to the interests of the United States in their connections with foreign powers." The military secretaries were "to superintend everything relating" to their respective departments, such as the "raising and equipping of troops, the care of military Stores, public Fortifications, arsenals, and the like," in the case of the one; and "the public ships, Dock-yards, naval stores, and Arsenals," in the case of the other. [36]

---

[35] For text of the resolution, see Farrand, Records, vol. ii, pp. 342–343.

[36] Ibid., vol. ii, pp. 342–343.

In short, Morris and Pinckney combined in an ambitious attempt to furnish a complete constitutional organization of national administration on the basis of complete ultimate control by the President.   The exclusion of the Senate from all participation in the matter of appointment and the inclusion of the tenure of offices provision could have been intended for no other purpose.   To be sure, the provisions were not included in the finished Constitution, which was undoubtedly a wise step.[37]   But this does not necessarily signify opposition to the basic idea, but rather a belief that the matter was properly one for legislative determination. One of the most important elements of the proposed plan, the presidential position of supremacy with respect to the departmental heads, is in fact inferable from the only clause retained.   Written opinions were to be required by the President, the superior, from the department heads, the inferiors, as the former desired.

It can not be denied that this concept of the President's control over the existing department chiefs entailed a very great extension of his personal power.   Those things which the plan empowered the subordinate secretaries to do became really an integral part of the presidential power.   This is particularly interesting as concerns foreign affairs, the control of which was then vested in the Senate.   Although treaties were to be made by the Senate, the preparation of plans for them was regarded as an executive function.   The same was true of the consideration of those made abroad and all correspondence.

Indeed, if there was in the minds of the delegates the thought that in the natural course of things the business of the departments was to be conducted under the general leadership of the President, we must extend the somewhat limited field of presidential power defined by the constitutional enumeration to include those things which were being done by the existing departments, in order to obtain a cor-

---

[37] For a discussion of this point as an abstract matter, see W. F. Willoughby, Government of Modern States, pp. 111–112.

rect idea of what the term signified, at least to that school
represented by Hamilton, Morris and Pinckney, and to a
majority of the delegates who sat as members of the first
Congress and voted for the uncontrolled executive power to
remove departmental heads.   This interpretation would ob-
viate the necessity of such juristic gymnastics as that which
derives the President's control over foreign affairs from his
powers to make treaties and to name and receive ambassadors—in the two first of which the Senate participates, and
the latter undoubtedly intended as a purely formal power.

From still another point of view this proposed council is
instructive.   Executive influence on legislative measures is
very generally spoken of as a modern development, entirely
unforeseen by the framers of the Constitution, pictured as
bound hand and foot by the doctrine of separation.   And
yet we see that the idea of executive preparation and report
of plans of legislation was very much alive.   The lessons
concerning the incompetence of a legislative body to legislate
were not forgotten, nor was the doctrine of separation so
far a master word as to negate their influence.

Another aspect of the matter has at least a speculative
interest, namely, the possible results of a constitutionally
created council with constitutionally guaranteed powers of
initiation of legislation, each member of which was to "be
responsible for his opinion on the affairs relating to his particular Department," when a matter was submitted for discussion by the council.   The idea of the irresponsible chief
magistrate was not involved, for the President was not
bound by his advice, nor indeed obliged to consult his council
at all.   The influence of the British executive organization is,
however, very plain, especially in the inclusion of the Chief
Justice in the Council as a kind of keeper of the public con-
science,[38] and the adoption of the plan would almost certainly

---

[38] He was to recommend measures "necessary to the due administration of Justice, and such as may promote useful learning and
inculcate sound morality throughout the Union" (Farrand, Records,
vol. ii, p. 335).

in practice have resulted in a diminution of the importance of the position of the President to the benefit of his subordinates.

Its failure marks the final elimination of the separate council idea, and *pro tanto* an abandonment of the English scheme of executive organization. Nor was it because of a failure to consider the proposition, resembling in some features at least the plan utilized in the mother country, but because of the danger involved in trying to combine the feature of conciliar advice with the responsible chief. As Gouverneur Morris said, in explaining the final omission:

> The question of a Council was considered in the Committee, where it was judged that the Presidt. by persuading his Council—to concur in his wrong measures would acquire their protection for them.[39]

The history of these proposals need not detain us. The Convention was more interested in finishing its work and going home than in considering new proposals. The plan, without discussion, was referred to the committee of detail,[40] which reported it back shorn of the organization provisions, but retaining those concerning the advisory council, to whose membership were added the speaker of the House and the president of the Senate.[41] There the matter rested, until the committee of eleven on unfinished business reported back the clause concerning the President's power to require advice in writing from the secretaries, a last feeble remnant of the British idea of the Council of the King, and an intentionally meaningless imitation of that ministerial countersignature of the acts of the irresponsible monarch, from which the British cabinet system has been derived.

The second of the chief points of interest above mentioned, the work of the committee of eleven, can not be treated without a brief chronological review of the action of the Convention on those parts of the report of the committee of detail

---

[39] Ibid., vol. ii, p. 542. Mercer of Maryland had urged a council " being members of both Houses " (Ibid., vol. ii. pp. 284–285.)

[40] Ibid., vol. ii, p. 342.

[41] Ibid., vol. ii, p. 367.

which concerned executive power. Following the order of the report, these were the eligibility of members of Congress to office, the veto power, the special powers of the Senate, and the executive article proper.

The first of these was reached August 14. There was quite a debate on the matter, in which the old ground was gone over without developing any new ideas. The feature of the debate was an extreme speech by Mercer of Maryland, who very explicitly stated that "governments can only be maintained by *force* or *influence,*" and that inasmuch as the executive had not force, to "deprive him of influence by rendering the members of the Legislature ineligible to Executive offices" was to reduce him to "a mere phantom of authority." [42]   No conclusion was reached, the whole matter being postponed pending a determination of the Senate's powers. [43]

The qualified veto provisions were the occasion of a fourth attempt by Madison and Wilson to join the Supreme Court to the President in the exercise of this power. [44]   The debate on this proposal raked over even mouldier straw than that on eligibility.   Mercer, Dickinson and Gouverneur Morris objected to the theory that judges could declare unconstitutional laws to be *ab initio* void, the latter, it is interesting to observe, on the ground that the judiciary was after all a part of the executive. [45]   Wilson took occasion to remind the Convention that "the prejudices agst the Executive resulted from a misapplication of the adage that the parliament was the palladium of liberty.   Where the Executive was really formidable, *King* and *Tyrant,* were naturally associated in the minds of the people; not *legislature* and *tyranny.*   But where the Executive was not formidable, the two last were most properly associated," [46] pointing his moral by reference to the

[42] Ibid., vol. ii, p. 284.
[43] Ibid., vol. ii, p. 290.   This is good proof that the action of the committee on this point did not meet with approval.
[44] See text of his resolution, Farrand, Records, vol. ii, pp. 294-295.
[45] Ibid., vol. ii, pp. 298-299.
[46] Ibid., vol. ii, pp. 300-301.

Long Parliament.   But the judges were excluded, though the proportion of votes required for repassage was raised to three fourths.   The succeeding day the veto power was extended to apply to " every order, resolution or vote," as well as to bills in order to prevent legislative evasion, on which occasion Sherman used language that indicated a belief, on his part at least, that the President should be allowed a veto on separate " votes taking money out of the Treasury." [47]

The debate on Congress's power to make war cast considerable light on the Convention's idea of the respective relation of the two departments to that phase of state activity. On motion of Madison " declare " was substituted for " make," as better " leaving to the Executive the power to repel sudden attacks " [48] and also because " make " " might be understood to ' conduct ' which was an Executive function." [49]

On August 23 the question of the Senate's special powers came before the Convention.   Indications had not been lacking that the conclusions of the committee of detail were not regarded as final.   Mercer had flatly stated that he did not believe that any save legislative powers should be assigned this branch,[50] and had expressly objected to associating the Senate in the business of treaty making which was, he claimed, properly an executive function, though adding that treaties would have to be ratified by the legislative authority before becoming laws of the land.[51]   As has been seen, the question of eligibility of members of Congress to office had gone over pending a final determination of the Senate's powers.   Williamson and Rutledge had also indicated a possibility of revision.[52]

On the other hand, there was a general realization that the Senate, with the powers it then possessed, was an executive

[47] Ibid., vol. ii, p. 405.
[48] Ibid., vol. ii, p. 318.
[49] Ibid., vol. ii, p. 319, Madison's footnote.
[50] Ibid., vol. ii, p. 259.
[51] Ibid., vol. ii, p. 257.
[52] Ibid., vol. ii, p. 297.

council, and would perhaps be in constant session. Madison and Rutledge had moved that the Senate, "when not in its Legislative capacity," be not compelled to publish a journal of its proceedings.[53] Gouverneur Morris had declared that the Senate would sit constantly.[54] Charles Pinckney spoke of the power of the Senate to make treaties and "manage foreign affairs." [55] Ghoram urged that senators' salaries should be higher than those of members of the House because they would "be detained longer from home, [and] obliged to remove their families, and in time of war perhaps to sit constantly." [56]

Success of the Wilson plan for the independent executive was plainly endangered. It is consequently no surprise to find both Wilson and Morris on their feet with the familiar protest against vesting the appointment of judges of the Supreme Court in the upper house.[57] Madison likewise "observed that the Senate represented the States alone, and that for this as well as obvious reasons it was proper that the President should be an agent in treaties." [58] Morris "did not know that he should refer the making of treaties to the Senate at all, but for the present wd. move to add as an amendment to the section, after 'treaties'—'but no treaty shall be binding on the U. S. which is not ratified by a law.' " [59]

This motion reveals much. It shows the dislike of the national group for the Senate as a representative of the States qua States, a determination on their part to pare down its special powers and to substitute therefor the influence of the more national House of Representatives and the equally national President, both of whom would necessarily participate in the passage of the ratifying act. Also there is involved in the motion the enhancement of large states' influence and the diminution of that of the small.

---

[53] Ibid., vol. ii, p. 259.
[54] Ibid., vol. ii, p. 224.
[55] Ibid., vol. ii, p. 235.
[56] Ibid., vol. ii, p. 293.
[57] Ibid., vol. ii, p. 389.
[58] Ibid., vol. ii, p. 392.
[59] Ibid., vol. ii, p. 392.

The debate on this motion is not illuminating. As did so many of the debates on treaty making, it went off on the subject of the relation of the power to make treaties and the law-making power, hinging on the point of whether a ratified treaty was of its own force the law of the land. One fact is revealed by it, however, namely, that the idea that the plenipotentiary, if he obeyed his instructions, bound the sovereign to ratify his acts had not been abandoned. Both Ghoram and Johnson objected to the motion, since, in the words of the latter, "there was something of solecism in saying that the acts of a minister with plenipotentiary powers from one Body, should depend for ratification on another body," while pointing out that the power of making treaties in Great Britain was completely vested in the Crown.[60]

The significance of this lies in the fact that it may be reasonably inferred that, when ultimately the President and Senate were joined in the exercise of the treaty-making power, it was intended that the instructions for plenipotentiaries should be jointly prepared, since otherwise the same "solecism" that was here objected to would exist. The value of this inference can not now be estimated. But the point of view indicated must be borne in mind.[61]

At any rate, the combination of small state votes with those determined by these, and other, considerations combined to defeat the proposal. Nevertheless, as Randolph pointed out, every one who spoke expressed dissatisfaction with the existing arrangement.[62] The Convention, while not decided as to what ought to be done, was unwilling to accept

---

[60] Ibid., vol. ii, pp. 392–393.

[61] And yet it is not true that the old Congress had invariably considered itself bound by the acts of its plenipotentiaries. I have found but one exception, but it is an important one. The plenipotentiaries—the term is retained in the commission—who were sent to Europe to make treaties of amity and commerce were empowered only "to . . . confer, treat and negotiate concerning . . . a treaty of amity and commerce . . ., to make and receive propositions for such treaty, and to conclude and sign the same, transmitting it to the United States in Congress assembled for their final ratification." See Journals of Congress. vol. iii, pp. 498–499.

[62] Farrand, Records, vol. ii, p. 393.

the committee's proposal for constituting the upper house a special council for exclusive control over foreign affairs. Nor was it willing at this stage of things to debate it further. Consequently, without objection, it was referred to the committee of detail, where it continued to rest until the committee of eleven on unfinished business took it under consideration.

On August 24 the executive article was taken up for discussion. The first change instituted was to provide that election of the President should be by joint ballot of the legislature, all the small States save New Hampshire voting against the proposal. A motion made to secure a vote by States, rather than by head, failed, though the support of Georgia was won over. New Hampshire again sacrificed her interest to the principle that "this general officer ought to be elected by the joint and general voice." [63]

No step more important than this in its ultimate effects on the executive department was taken by the Convention. Georgia, South Carolina and North Carolina had stood as a solid phalanx for the principle of legislative election. Pennsylvania and Virginia, despite the opposition of Mason and Randolph, had been the backbone of the independent executive movement. Massachusetts had on several occasions displayed a tendency to repudiate the electoral idea. The small States thus still possessed the balance of power.

The small States had, as has been noted, as a whole shown no hostility to the principle of a non-legislative source of election. When the matter was before the Convention in July, they had on one occasion voted as a unit with Pennsylvania and Virginia for choice by electors. The influence that had then finally put enough of them on the side of choice by the legislature had been the factor of representation. Now, with one fell blow, they were deprived of almost all of the advantage they had hoped to win through legislative choice. The time was ripe for the strong executive forces to act.

As was to be expected, the astute Morris was immediately

---

[63] Ibid., vol. ii, p. 402.

in the breach with a proposition for choice by electors to be chosen by the people.   Although popular choice of the electors savoured strongly of large state control, New Jersey, Delaware and Connecticut joined Pennsylvania and Virginia, only to lose by a single vote.[64]   On the abstract question of choice by electors, the vote, taken in what was evidently a thin house, was a tie, four States to four, with two divided and one absent.[65]   Whereupon the matter went over, on the insistence, significantly, of New Jersey.

The remainder of the debate on the executive provision is of no great interest.   An attempt made by Sherman to give the legislature the power to determine how offices created by law were to be filled was overwhelmingly defeated, showing how completely the Convention had gotten away from the idea of controlling the executive through ordinary law.[66]   On motion of Madison, "offices" was substituted for "officers" in the appointing clause, in order to make it plain that the right to create offices was a legislative one.   Sherman's motion to join the Senate in the exercise of the pardon power was defeated, Connecticut alone supporting it.[67]   Having postponed the method of impeachment question, the Convention proceeded to adopt the enumeration of powers, and then, despite the unfinished condition of the executive, passed to a consideration of other matters.

Thus, as late as August 31, the method of election of the chief magistrate, the question of eligibility to reëlection, the degree of participation by Senate and President respectively in control of foreign affairs and the naming of judges, the method of impeachment, succession in case of vacancies, and the matter of a council were all yet unsettled.   Consequently, on this date the Convention had recourse to the increasingly popular expedient of creating a committee to expedite mat-

[64] Ibid., vol. ii, p. 402.

[65] Ibid., vol. ii, p. 402.   Massachusetts was absent, and Connecticut and Maryland divided.   Evidently, either Ellsworth or Johnson had left the hall.

[66] Ibid., vol. ii, p. 405.

[67] Ibid., vol. ii, p. 419.

ters. To it was referred all unfinished business, which meant for the most part the executive provisions, but included the much-mooted question of the exclusive right of the lower house to initiate financial measures, and the question of the eligibility of members of Congress to national office. The members of the committee were Gilman, King, Sherman, Brearley, Gouverneur Morris, Dickinson, Carroll, Madison, Williamson, Butler and Baldwin. Manifestly it was this committee that organized the executive, as it was the committee of detail that enumerated its powers. If it could work out a compromise, it was a foregone conclusion that the Convention would accept it.

On September 1 the committee reported on the question of eligibility of members of Congress to office. The report was a victory for the anti-executives, for it provided that no member should be eligible for office during his term, and no officer could be a member of the legislature unless he resigned his office.[68] On September 3 the report was debated and amended so as to take its present form, the ineligibility being to offices " created or the emoluments whereof shall have been increased " during the member's term of office.[69]

On September 4 reports were made on the remaining points. Briefly, it was provided that impeachments should be tried by the Senate, a two-thirds vote being necessary to convict. The President was to hold office for four years, without restriction as to eligibility. He was to be chosen by an electoral college, composed of electors chosen in each State in such manner as the state legislature should determine, a majority of electoral votes being required for choice. If no candidate had such a majority, the Senate was to choose from the five highest candidates. The requirement was inserted that the President be a natural-born citizen or a citizen of the United States at the time of the adoption of the Constitution.

---

[68] Ibid., vol. ii, p. 483.
[69] Ibid., vol. ii, pp. 491–492. The significance of this was that it allowed a member to resign his seat and immediately accept an office, rather than being obliged to wait until the expiration of his term.

Provision was made for a vice-president, to be president of the Senate, and to succeed to the presidency in case of a vacancy. Treaties were to be made by the President, by and with the advice and consent of two thirds of the Senate, and the President was to nominate all officers, including ambassadors and judges of the Supreme Court, subject to approval by a majority of the Senate. The President was empowered to call for the opinion in writing of the executive department heads " upon any subject relating to the duties of their respective offices." Impeachment was to be on conviction for treason or bribery.[70] On the following day the committee further reported a clause restoring the exclusive origination of money bills in the House.[71]

Thus finally the second element of the Wilson plan, namely, choice by an organ independent of the legislature and somewhat approaching popular election, obtained its place in the Constitution, but not without payment, for the small States had demanded and obtained their pound of flesh. Choice by electors had first to be made more attractive to them than choice by the legislature. This was done by providing that in the electoral college voting should be in the same proportion as on joint ballot, while in case no majority was obtained in the electoral vote, the Senate should elect from the five highest candidates. Since there was no foreknowledge of the effect that the party system was destined to have on the choice of Presidents, the second provision was regarded as a real gain.[72]

---

[70] Ibid., vol. ii, pp. 497–499.

[71] Ibid., vol. ii, pp. 508–509.

[72] Morris long after the Convention declared: " the necessity of voting for two persons for President, one of whom should not be of the State voting, and the right of choosing a President out of the five highest on the list, where no absolute choice was made by the electors, is perhaps the most valuable provision in favor of the small States, which can be found in the Constitution." Gouverneur Morris to L. R. Morris, December 10, 1803, Farrand, Records, vol. iii, p. 405. Butler claimed in the Senate that another reason for the provision concerning the two highest candidates was " to prevent the putting up of any powerful man." Ibid., vol. iii, p. 404. He also claimed to have been the author of the whole electoral provision.

As a bid it was completely successful. Every small State except New Hampshire voted against the proposal to return to the original plan, and the latter State was divided,[73] and, in the end, voted for the plan as recommended.[74] The Carolina delegates alone remained irreconcilable.

Not only were the small States satisfied by this arrangement, but in a most unobtrusive fashion the three-fifths compromise was carried over into the election of the executive, thus satisfying the Southern States without unduly parading the fact. Even the peculiar internal situation in South Carolina, where the "low country" minority controlled the legislature, was recognized by the clause which left the method of choice of the electors to the state legislature, a clause which that State utilized to its fullest by maintaining choice by the legislature until the outbreak of the Civil War. And above all "the indispensable necessity of making the Executive independent of the Legislature" was satisfied, and the many who "were anxious even for an immediate choice by the people" given a half loaf, which was ultimately to become a full one.[75]

The relation of the Senate to executive business was settled after the same give and take fashion. What the President gained in control of foreign affairs and appointment of judges, he lost in making other appointments. The gain in the first-named instance was a tremendous one. Whatever the assumption made concerning the relation of the President to the secretary of foreign affairs, the fact remained that he had only a mere vestige of explicit constitutional power in that field. The change embodied in the compromise plan confined the participation of the Senate in foreign affairs entirely to treaties. Its control over ambassadors was now

P. Butler to W. Butler, May 5, 1788, ibid., vol. iii, p. 302. The provisions were, however, for the most part dictated by the existing situation. Indeed, almost every part of it had been already suggested in the Convention.

[73] Farrand, Records, vol. ii, p. 511.

[74] Ibid., vol. ii, p. 525.

[75] The quotations are from Morris's explanation of the motives which governed the committee. Farrand, Records, vol. ii, p. 500.

placed on the same basis as its control over any other officer, rather than on that of general senatorial control over their field of activity. In other words, the change marked an elimination of the idea to which Pinckney had given expression that the Senate was. "to have the power of making treaties and managing our foreign affairs," [76] and the substitution of the much narrower concept that the Senate should advise in making treaties, and in naming ambassadors. Since nothing was said concerning the general management of foreign affairs, the way was left clear for its exercise as a normal executive function with results that are well known.

Nor, we may believe, could the adherents of executive strength have foreseen that the power to negative appointments given the Senate would, through the instrumentality of an extra-constitutional convention, and one, too, in manifest contravention of its spirit, become the distributor of a large part of domestic patronage. Clinton's control of nominations had given him control of the patronage, as was well known to all conversant with New York politics. It may be surmised that it was thought that the proposal would work the same way under the new instrument.

Even the last portion of the report of the committee, that which dealt with money bills, was utilized, chiefly by Morris, we may think, as a part of the general plan to further, so far as possible, executive independence and strength. This provision was naturally no favorite of the small States. Also the clearer thinkers of the large state delegations had sufficient insight to see that what had been the chief weapon of the House of Commons against an hereditary House of Lords and an irresponsible executive chief had no raison d'être in the American system. But, as Madison observed, "Col. Mason, Mr. Gerry and other members from large States see great value on this privilege of originating money bills. Of this the members from the small States, with some from the large States who wished a high mounted Govt., endeavored

[76] Ibid., vol. ii, p. 235.

to avail themselves, by making that privilege, the price of arrangements in the constitution favorable to the small States, and to the elevation of the Government." [77]

It was shrewd trading, after all, by shrewd politicians that determined this great settlement, and it requires no great stretch of the imagination to reconstruct a picture of Mr. Gouverneur Morris, aided perhaps by King, fresh from his triumph in the matter of navigation acts and the slave trade, obtained chiefly by keeping the Southern delegates on tenterhooks by extreme speeches on slavery, ably manipulating the resources available to the friends of a "high mounted government." It is not only the fact that Morris explains the action of the committee to the Convention, and later defends it against his colleague Wilson, but the extreme astuteness of the bargaining that gives it the impress of his handiwork.

Nevertheless the compromise arrangements were a bitter draught for the first sponsor of the independent executive idea, James Wilson. The whole scheme he said had "a dangerous tendency to aristocracy, as throwing dangerous power into the hands of the Senate." That body would have, he claimed, in reality the appointment of the President, and through that control of appointments. It was also to make treaties and try impeachments. "According to the plan as it now stands, the President will not be the man of the people as he ought to be, but the Minion of the Senate." [78] The division of powers indeed struck at the root of Wilson's concept of personal presidential responsibility. "Good laws," he declared, "are of no effect without a good Executive; and there can be no good Executive without a responsible appointment of officers to execute. Responsibility is in a manner destroyed by such an agency as the Senate." [79]

But, as Morris pointed out, the stronger executives had gotten enough to satisfy them, certainly, we may be sure, as

---

[77] Ibid., vol. ii, p. 515. Madison's note. See Morris's remarks, pp. 509–510.
[78] Ibid., vol. ii, pp. 522–523.
[79] Ibid., vol. ii, pp. 538–539.

much as was possible. The Senate had lost its exclusive power to appoint judges, it did not gain any new powers over treaties, and it lost the right to participate directly in the election of the President in the first instance. As for appointments, "the weight of sentiment in the House was opposed to the exercise of it by the President alone."[80]

None the less a general feeling existed that the Senate was too strong, and Williamson's suggestion that election in those cases where no majority of electors was obtained be decided by the House voting by States was readily adopted.[81]

There was, however, no real chance to upset the foundations of the compromise. The fact that the Convention stood at the threshold of freedom was the strongest defence the new plan could have. By accepting it the way was cleared for the final action—the putting of the instrument into its final form and ratification.

One part of the committee's report, it should be noted, was entirely new, namely, that part which required the chief magistrate to be a natural-born citizen of the United States, or a citizen at the time of the adoption of the convention. Its inclusion seems to have been determined by a letter from Jay to Washington—he may have written to others—in which he wrote as follows:

Permit me to hint whether it would not be wise and seasonable to provide a strong check to the admission of Foreigners into the administration of our national Government, and to declare expressly that the Command in chief of the American army shall not be given to, nor devolve on, any but a natural born citizen.[82]

The name of von Steuben is not mentioned, but there can be little doubt that it was he, 'alieni appetens, sui profusus,' with his sympathies for the followers of Shay, and his evidently suspected dealings with Prince Henry of Prussia, whom Jay had in mind when he penned these words. The silent insertion of the clause in a committee where matters could be managed quietly tends to confirm the conjecture.[83]

---

[80] Ibid., vol. ii, p. 524.
[81] Ibid., vol. ii, p. 527.
[82] Jay to Washington, July 25, 1787, ibid., vol. iii, p. 61.
[83] Apparently von Steuben was not a citizen of the United States

The next stage in the work of the Convention was to give the Constitution its final literary polish. Consequently, on September 8 a committee was chosen consisting of Johnson, Hamilton, Gouverneur Morris, Madison and King "to revise the stile of and arrange the articles which had been agreed to by the House." This work was entrusted to Morris. On its face, there was nothing that this committee could do to affect the nature of any of the constitutional provisions. And yet a shrewd man by choice of phraseology could do much. He could, on his own admission, phrase the articles on admission of new States so as to confine it to territory already within the territorial limits of the United States.[84] He could, again on his own admission, use language concerning the judiciary which while "expressing my own notions would not alarm others, nor shock their self love."[85] He could indeed be charged with attempting at the last moment to change the national government into one of unenumerated powers by setting off the "general welfare" description of the objects of national taxation as a separate clause.[86] Positively with respect to the executive article he could do nothing. But he could do much by leaving the vesting clause as it stood.

When the report of the committee of style was submitted it was found that the legislative grant now read: "All legislative powers herein granted shall be vested in a Congress." That the judicial power should be understood as similarly completely described by the enumeration was secured by utilizing the phrase "the judicial power shall extend to," the enumeration ensuing. But the executive power was vested in the old way: "the executive power shall be vested in a President of the United States of America."

In modern parlance, this phrase was to prove a "joker."

and so was not exempted by the proviso exempting persons already citizens.

[84] G. Morris to H. W. Livingston, December 4, 1803, Farrand, Records, vol. iii, p. 404.
[85] G. Morris to Pickering, December 22, 1814, ibid., vol. ii, p. 419.
[86] Gallatin, in the House, June 19, 1798, ibid., vol. ii, p. 379.

That it was retained by Morris with full realization of its possibilities the writer does not doubt.   At any rate, whether intentional or not, it admitted an interpretation of executive power which would give to the President a field of action much wider than that outlined by the enumerated powers. With the correctness or incorrectness of this interpretation we are not concerned.   The results of such a possibility were far reaching.

The presidential article was now complete save for two last-minute changes.   The proportion of votes necessary for repassage of a law, raised to three fourths when the President was elected by the legislature, was now changed to two thirds,[87] and a clause was inserted giving Congress the right to vest the appointment of inferior officers in the President alone or in the heads of the departments.   With these changes it was laid before the people of the respective States for their adoption.

---

[87] Farrand, Records, vol. ii, p. 587.

CHAPTER VI

The Removal Debate

The completion of Article II of the Constitution seems, at first sight, a logical place for an evaluation of the work of the Convention and an interpretation of the executive established by it. A closer view reveals the fact that such an evaluation and interpretation is hardly possible. Rushed through in the last days of the Convention's being, as much of it was, the executive article fairly bristles with contentious matter, and, until it is seen what decision was given to these contentions, it is impossible to say just what the national executive meant.

It is impossible, for example, if recourse be had to the bare words of the Constitution alone, to determine what were the intended relations of the Senate to executive business. Was its participation in the appointment of all executive officers to entitle it to a participation in their control, thus constituting it a general executive council with a peculiar interest in administrative business? Did its participation in the naming of ambassadors and in the ratification—or, as it is claimed, the making—of treaties entitle it to be informed of all important transactions in the field of foreign affairs? What of the question that has just necessitated the above double form of statement? Is the Senate a treaty-making or a treaty-ratifying body?

Again, nothing is more vital than the relations of the executive head to the chief officers of the administrative departments, and the relations of the latter to the legislature. And yet the Constitution furnishes no final and authoritative decision of the question. It was doubtless in accord with sound principles of constitutional drafting to leave to the legislature the actual organization of the organs of administration. But when the Constitution failed even to decide the fundamental question of whether the legislature or the chief executive was their master, it results that it was hardly possible to speak of the executive as completed.

The debates in the Convention do not afford an answer to these questions. As to the administrative headship of the President, we have found evidence enough to upset the interpretation usually given that this silence of the Constitution indicates a complete failure to envisage the President in such a capacity, and enough to forecast the decision which would, in due time, be given it. As to the intended relations of the Senate and the executive under the final plan, the evidence is even scantier. There was neither time nor desire to discuss the compromise fully, nor opportunity to discuss it at all on its merits. It was accepted as it came from the committee, without any real effort to determine what its more remote implications were.

But, it may be objected, if any consideration is given to the operations of the new government, where will be the stopping point? Because of the peculiar relations of the courts to the executive, the actual relations of the two political departments to each other have been the product of a political development which continues even to the present. Is it justifiable to say arbitrarily, here we stop in our study of this process and declare that this is the executive as intended by the men who made the Constitution?

It is believed that these objections can be satisfactorily met, if the end of the first session of the first Congress be taken as the stopping point. This for three reasons. In the first place, when this Congress in its first session organized the administrative departments, it was sitting as a constitutional convention, so far as subject matter is a criterion, just as certainly as the Convention, *par excellence,* was. In fact, its work was simply a continuation of that done in Philadelphia two years before. Again, in the two houses of the legislature there were no fewer than eighteen former members of the Convention, eight in the House, including Madison, whose leadership there, not yet threatened by the Secretary of the Treasury, is unmistakable, and in the Senate ten, exactly one half of its membership.[1] A roster of these members shows that included in this eighteen were some of the most influential of the Convention delegates. They were, in the House, Baldwin, Carroll, Clymer, Fitzsimons, Gerry, Gilman, Madison, and Sherman; in the Senate, Langdon, Strong, Ellsworth, Johnson, Paterson, Robert Morris, Bassett, Read, Butler, and Few.[2] If a majority of these men are found participating in the decision of a majority of Congress, the assumption of the identity of this opinion with that of the Convention is greatly strengthened. In the last place, the political environment, so to speak, of this first session of Congress was the same as that of the Convention, a state of affairs which was not to endure for long. No new political and social influences had arisen to align man in different groups from those of 1787. Hamilton's financial measures, the rise of the Anglo-French question, and Jefferson's assumption of leadership of the opposition, with one of the chief planks in his platform opposition to extension of executive power, were soon to modify the existing grouping, forcing Madison, for example, into the anti-national party, Luther Martin into the national party. But in 1789 the former delegates to the Convention brought to New York the same political beliefs and political prejudices that they had carried with them from Philadelphia.

There is one objection that can not be completely answered. In the Convention voting was by States. In Congress the case was quite otherwise. But inasmuch as every State which was represented had in its delegation at least one former Convention member,[3] and inasmuch as the absence of

---

[1] Subsequently, when New York was represented, the number was eleven, the proportion of course being the same. King was the New York senator who had sat in the Convention.

[2] There were fifty-five members who at one time or another attended the Convention.

[3] The geographical distribution was, Georgia, 2; Maryland, 1; Pennsylvania, 3; Massachusetts, 2; New Hampshire, 2; Virginia, 1;

anti-nationalists and believers in a weak executive such as
Martin, Bedford, Rutledge, and Randolph was more than
counterbalanced by the absence of Hamilton, Wilson, Gouverneur Morris, King and Charles Pinckney, it does not seem
that the assumption of general identity of opinion can be
refuted.

The portion of the work of the first session of the first
Congress which most directly concerns the present study is,
of course, the organization of the departments of war, of
foreign affairs and of the treasury. Granted that this action
may be considered in a study of origins, no doubt can arise
as to its importance in explaining the real meaning of the
solution given the executive problem by the Constitution.
The question of the relation of the President to the heads of
the departments was settled with as much finality as a legislative interpretation could, thereby eliminating all possibilities
of a political control of the executive officers by the legislature either as a whole or through either of its houses. At
the same time the seal of legislative disapproval was set on
the concept of a Senate acting as a general council for administrative affairs. Also, the debates that were precipitated
by these measures throw much light on the still unsettled
question of the proper degree of senatorial participation in
the general business of foreign affairs, and the special field
of treaty making. Even from the strictly juristic point of
view, the action is interesting, for, so far as joint action by
legislature and executive could, it established clearly at least
one principle of constitutional interpretation of far-reaching
significance.

As is well known, the point at issue in the determination
of this question of the organization of the departments was
whether or not the President should possess the sole power
to remove the heads of these departments from office. As
is equally well known, the result was a determination to include in each measure a phrase which would indicate the leg-

---

Connecticut, 3; New Jersey, 1; Delaware, 2; South Carolina, 1;
New York was represented in the House, but not yet in the Senate.

islative opinion that this power was vested in the President by the Constitution. The provision was identical in each of the three organization bills.

This result was reached, however, only after a prolonged struggle in which widely differing constitutional interpretations were put forward. In all, four distinct theories concerning the power of removal were advanced: that the major executive officers held office on good behavior and were removable only by impeachment; that the power to remove was incident to the power to appoint, was consequently vested by the Constitution jointly in the President and Senate, and should be left unmentioned in the organization bills, or, if mentioned, should be recognized as possessed jointly; that the power to create offices was complete, and included a right on the part of Congress to vest removal where it chose, which should be the President alone; finally, that the President possessed the sole power by virtue of the Constitution itself.

In view of the fact that the failure of Congress to denominate the treasury department "executive" in the title to the act creating it and to include a clause especially empowering the President to direct and control the secretary in the discharge of his duties has been quite generally interpreted as final proof that the President was regarded as the directing, controlling head only of those departments whose duties lay in the fields peculiarly presidential in character, it may be well to emphasize the fact that the debate was on the right to remove, that this right extended to all three departments, and that the principles determining the ultimate decision were of a general character, applying to all administrative business alike. To be sure, in every instance debate was precipitated on the removal of the secretary of foreign affairs. But as was pointed out at the time, this was merely shrewd parliamentary tactics.[4]

---

[4] "The committee have taken care to bring in the present bill," Representative Jackson pointed out, "previous to the bill for organization of the Treasury, that the principle might be established before that more delicate business came into view" (Annals of Congress, 1789–1791, vol. i, p. 550. Cited as Annals, vol. 1).

The first of the above-mentioned theories concerning the power of removal is interesting chiefly because of its possibilities, for it secured few adherents. The fundamental practical objection to it was the difficulty of getting rid of an incompetent or corrupt officer. The constitutional argument was that the express provision of tenure on good behavior for the judiciary was to be interpreted as excluding such tenure for all officers for whom such express provision was not made. This interpretation was accepted, and it was very generally agreed that the power to remove was somewhere in the government.

There is no evidence that the House realized the full importance of this action.[5] To have declared the magistracy permanent except for the right of removal by impeachment would necessarily have made the department heads the real executive. An incoming President would have found in office men whose position, so far as he was concerned, was assured. They would have ideas of their own and connections of their own. Since he could not control them, they would very naturally act in accordance with these ideas in carrying out their duties. On the other hand, Congress would have been forced to use the weapon of impeachment as a means of political control. It is extremely probable that very soon some more easily worked system of control would have been evolved, with the result that responsibility would have been to the legislature. This, of course, would have meant some sort of ministerial government. The refusal of the House to accept the argument that the only way under the Constitution to get rid of a minister was a legislative process in which the lower House would take the initiative was, consciously or not, a refusal to establish ministerial government, with all that this entailed.[6]

---

[5] But see Madison's remarks on the practical effects of joining the Senate in the power to remove, Annals, vol. i, pp. 162–163; see below, p. 149.

[6] This is predicated on the assumption that irremovable officers would sooner or later have found themselves out of harmony with an incoming President.

The supporters of senatorial participation in removal had a strong case. Their argument was a simple one. It was well and briefly expressed by Gerry, who, with Sherman, furnished the only support the doctrine received in the House from former members of the Convention. He expressed his position as follows:

> The constitution provides for the appointment of the public officers in this manner: (quoting the relevant clause of the Constitution.) Now, if there be no other clause respecting the appointment, I shall be glad to see how the heads of departments are to be removed by the President alone. What clause is it that gives this power in express terms? I believe there is none such. If there is a power of removal, besides that by impeachment, it must rest somewhere. It must rest in the President, or in the President and Senate, or in the President, Senate, and House of Representatives. Now, there is no clause which expressly vests in the President. I believe no gentleman contends it is in this House,[7] because that would be that mingling of the executive and legislative powers gentlemen deprecate. I presume, then, gentlemen will grant, that if there is such a power, it vests with the President, by and with the advice and consent of the Senate, who are the body who appoints.[8]

Whatever was the difference in the constitutional arguments of opponents to this position, they were in agreement as to its inexpediency. It is in their objections on this score that the concept of the President as responsible head of all the departments, and hence of administration, is most clearly revealed. The correlative unwillingness to see the Senate act as an executive council participating in the business of administration is made equally clear. Waiving for the moment the question of constitutionality, we may notice some of the more important of these practical arguments.

The opinion of Madison is, of course, of the greatest importance. He urged strongly the necessity of administrative integration in order to secure full executive responsibility, in words that leave not the shadow of a doubt that he thought of the President as the responsible head of administration. He declared:

> It is one of the most prominent features of the constitution, a principle that pervades the whole system, that there should be the

---

[7] Gerry probably said, and certainly meant, the whole legislature.
[8] Annals, vol. i, pp. 395–396.

highest possible degree of responsibility in all the executive officers thereof; any thing, therefore, which tends to lessen this responsibility, is contrary to its spirit and intention, and, unless it is saddled upon us expessly by the letter of that work, I shall oppose the admission of it into any act of the Legislature. Now, if the heads of the executive departments [9] are subjected to removal by the President alone, we have in him security for the good behavior of the officer. If he does not conform to the judgment of the President in doing the executive duties of his office, he can be displaced. This makes him responsible to the great executive power, and makes the President responsible to the public for the conduct of the person he has nominated and appointed to aid him in the administration of his department.[10]

And again:

If the President should possess alone the power of removal from office, those who are employed in the execution of the law will be in their proper situation, and the chain of dependence be preserved; the lowest officers, the middle grade, and the highest, will depend, as they ought, on the President, and the President on the community. The chain of dependence therefore terminates in the supreme body, namely in the people, who will possess, besidees, in aid of their original power the decisive engine of impeachment.[11]

Fisher Ames gave an equally lucid exposition of this view:

The constitution places all executive power in the hands of the President, and could he personally execute all the laws, there would be no occasion for auxiliaries; but the circumscribed powers of human nature in one man, demand the aid of others. When the objects are widely stretched, or greatly diversified, meandering through such an extent of territory as that the United States possess, a minister cannot see with his own eyes every transaction, or feel with his hands the minutiæ that pass through his department. He must therefore have assistants. But in order that he may be responsible to his country, he must have a choice in selecting his assistants, a control over them, with power to remove them when he finds the qualifications which induced their appointment to cease.

The executive powers are delegated to the President, with a view to have a responsible officer to superintend, control, inspect, and check the officers necessarily employed in administering the laws. The only bond between him and those he employs, is the confidence he has in their integrity and talents; when that confidence ceases, the principal ought to have power to remove those whom he can no longer trust with safety.[12]

---

[9] It should be noted that at this stage of the debate all the departments were denominated executive. The expression being dropped out by the committee that framed the bill. See the resolutions submitted to the committee, Annals, vol. i, p. 412.

[10] Annals, vol. i, p. 394.

[11] Ibid., vol. i, p. 518.

[12] Ibid., vol. i, pp. 492–493.

Indications are not lacking, indeed, that the magistracy, as it was called, was considered by some as a permanent body. Madison declared that a wanton removal of executive heads would be cause for impeachment,[13] and did not contemplate the dismissal of " a meritorious and virtuous officer." [14] But a very different view was expressed by Lawrence of New York, who said:

> It has been said by some gentlemen . . . that there may be a change of officers, and a complete revolution throughout the whole executive department, upon the election of every new President. I admit this may be the case, and contend that it should be the case, if the President thinks it necessary. I contend, that every President ought to have those men about him in whom he can place the most confidence, provided the Senate approve his choice. But we are not from hence to infer, that changes will be made in a wanton manner, and from capricious motives; . . . it may be fairly presumed, that changes will be made on principles of policy and propriety only.[15]

It is also true that the special relation of the offices of secretary of foreign affairs and that of war was mentioned in the debate. " The Departments of Foreign Affairs and War are peculiarly within the powers of the President," one member pointed out, "and he must be responsible for them." [16] But others were equally ready to infer a special relation for the Senate. Stone of Maryland argued as follows:

> As [the constitution] has given the power of making treaties, and judging of them, to the Senate and President, I should be inclined to believe, that as they have an immediate concern in and control over this business, they therefore ought to have the power of removal. It may be said, with respect to some other officers, that, agreeable to this principle, the President alone ought to have the sole power of removal; because he is interested in it, and has the control over the business they manage. For example, take the Minister at War. The President is commander-in-chief of the army and militia of the United States; but the ground is narrowed by the Senate being combined with him in making treaties; though here again the ground is reduced, because of the power combined in the whole Legislature to declare war and grant supplies.[17]

---

13 Ibid., vol. i, p. 517.
14 Ibid., vol. i, p. 518.
15 Ibid., vol. i, p. 504. Cf. pp. 511, 542.
16 Ibid., vol. i, p. 532.
17 Ibid., vol. i, p. 512.

But there was no disposition on the part of the proponents of presidential removal to rely on the argument of special relation to enumerated powers. Rather, so far as expediency was concerned, it was on the basis of the general control which the President should possess over the whole of the administrative organization that they rested their case. It was with full realization that control followed removal, and indeed for the specific purpose that it might, that such power was admitted to be in the President.

The natural corollary of this argument was the exclusion of the Senate from administrative business. The dangers of senatorial participation in the control of executive officers were pointed out by no one more trenchantly than by Madison:

Is there no danger that an officer, when he is appointed by the concurrence of the Senate, and has friends in that body, may choose rather to risk his establishment on the favor of that branch, than rest it upon the discharge of his duties to the satisfaction of the executive branch, which is constitutionally authorized to inspect and control his conduct? And if it should happen that the officers connect themselves with the Senate, they may mutually support each other, and for want of efficacy reduce the power of the President to a mere vapor; in which case, his responsibility would be annihilated, and the expectation of it unjust. The high executive officers, joined in cabal with the Senate, would lay the foundation of discord, and end in an assumption of the executive power, only to be removed by a revolution in the Government.[18]

In fact, Madison had no desire to see the Senate regarded as an executive council at all. The definiteness with which the issue was drawn may again best be shown by his own words. Mr. Madison, the record runs:

Begged his colleague (Mr. Bland) to consider the inconvenience his doctrine would occasion, by keeping the Senate constantly sitting in order to give their assent to the removal of an officer; they might see there would be a constant probability of the Senate being called upon to exercise this power, consequently they could not be a moment absent. Now, he did not believe the constitution imposed any such duty upon them.[19]

18 Ibid., vol. i, p. 480.
19 Ibid., vol. i, p. 390.

To which Bland replied that:

He did not think this objection of any weight, because the constitution made some other things their duty, which would require them to be pretty constantly sitting. He alluded to the part they were called upon to perform in making treaties; this, therefore, would be a trifling objection.[20]

The final action taken by the House can thus be interpreted in no other sense than to mean that, so far as was possible, the majority wished to give an unmistakable quietus to the idea, not unnatural in itself, and certainly held by some, that the two clauses allowing senatorial participation in executive matters constituted the Senate a permanent executive council, or, in fact, that it was an executive council at all.   There was equally, as Madison's remarks showed, a keen apprehension of creating any approximation to ministerial responsibility to the upper chamber, a result which would follow almost inevitably from allowing the Senate to control removals.

The majority who opposed joining the Senate in removals were thus as one in considering the President as the head of administration with full power to superintend, direct and control all subordinates.   They differed, however, with respect to the constitutional basis of their position.   One group claimed that the Constitution conferred the power on the President.   The other maintained that it was in the power of Congress to vest it where it chose.

The chief support of the latter was the clause empowering Congress to "make all laws which shall be necessary and proper for carrying into execution . . . all . . . powers vested by this constitution . . . in any department or officers." [21]   This, it was claimed, gave Congress full power to control everything incident to the creation of an office, including tenure.   Tenure, it was argued, might be fixed at a term of years, good behavior, or the will of the President, as Congress chose.   All, however, who held this view main-

[20] Ibid., vol. i, p. 397.
[21] Article I, sec. 8, clause 17.

tained that the power should be vested in the President.[22] Also, as one of their leaders, Sedgewick of Massachusetts, said of himself, there can be little doubt that they believed " it was more plausibly contended that the power of removal was more constitutionally in the President, than in the President and Senate; but . . . did not say that the arguments on either side were conclusive," [23] for, in the end, they voted as a unit for a bill that left no doubt that the power was the President's by virtue of the Constitution.

There were open to the " constitutional grant " adherents two methods of reasoning. Either they could fall back on the general executive grant and claim that the power to remove was an executive power, and hence vested in the President, or they could seek to interpret the appointing clause in such a way as to support them. In fact, they did both, but it was the former argument to which their chief appeal was made.

This argument was given its first and briefest statement by Clymer at the very outset of the debate, at a time when Madison was relying rather on the legislative grant idea:

The power of removal was an executive power, and as such belonged to the President, by the express words of the constitution: " the executive power shall be vested in a President of the United States of America." The Senate were not an executive body; they were a legislative one. It was true, in some instances, they held a qualified check over the executive power, but that was in consequence of an express declaration in the Constitution; without such declaration, they would not have been called upon for advice and consent in the case of appointment.[24]

This was the view that Madison ultimately held. He developed it to its fullest extent in the following language:

I have, since the subject was last before the House, examined the constitution with attention, and I acknowledge that it does not perfectly correspond with the ideas I entertained of it from the first glance. I am inclined to think, that a free and systematic interpretation of the plan of Government will leave us less liberty to abate the responsibilities than gentlemen imagine. I have already ac-

[22] See, for example, Sedgewick, Annals, vol. i, p. 541.
[23] Annals, vol. i, p. 565.
[24] Ibid., vol. i, pp. 396–397.

knowledged that the powers of the Government must remain as apportioned by the constitution.

The constitution affirms that the executive power shall be vested in the President. Are there exceptions to this proposition? Yes, there are. The constitution says, that in appointing to office the Senate shall be associated with the President, unless in the case of inferior officers, where the law shall otherwise direct. Have we a right to extend this exception? I believe not. If the constitution has invested all executive power in the President, I venture to assert that the Legislature has no right to diminish or modify his executive authority.

The question now resolves itself into this, Is the power of displacing an executive power? I conceive that if any power whatsoever is in its nature executive, it is the power of appointing, overseeing, and controlling those who execute the laws. If the constitution had not qualified the power of the President in appointing to office, by associating the Senate with him in that business, would it not be clear that he would have the right, by virtue of his executive power to make such appointment? Should we be authorized, in defiance of that clause in the constitution,—" The executive power shall be vested in a President,"—to unite the Senate with the President in the appointment to office? I conceive not. If it is admitted that we should not be authorized to do this, I think it may be disputed whether we have a right to associate them in removing persons from office, the one power being as much of an executive nature as the other.[25]

Nor was he willing to accept the doctrine of legislative control. That Congress participated in the business of administration he admitted, but only to a certain point:

The powers relative to officers are partly legislative and partly executive. The Legislature creates the office, defines the powers, limits its duration, and annexes a compensation. This done, the legislative power ceases.[26]

Only one officer was he willing to except from the general rule, the comptroller, who, he argued, partook of a judicial as well as an executive character.[27] The complete understanding of the application of the principle to all administrative officers is well evidenced by the fact that this attempt met with successful opposition on the grounds " that a majority of the House had decided that all officers concerned in executive business should depend upon the will of the President for their continuance in office; and with good

[25] Ibid., vol. i, pp. 481–482.
[26] Ibid., vol. i, p. 604.
[27] Ibid., vol. i, pp. 635–636.

reason, for they were the eyes and arms of the principal Magistrate, the instruments of execution." [28]

Despite their reliance on the general grant of executive power, this group, of whom Madison was the chief spokesman, were ready to meet their opponents on the ground of the language of the enumerated powers. Despite the participation of the Senate in the business of appointment, they argued that it was not an executive body. Advice and consent was an external, non-executive function. Not only nomination, but appointment also, was fundamentally the act of the executive. This position was expressed by Ames as follows:

It is doubted whether the Senate do actually appoint or not. It is admitted that they may check and regulate the appointment by the President, but they can do nothing more; they are merely an advisory body, and do not secure any degree of responsibility, which is one great object of the present constitution. . . . The President, I contend, has expressly the power of nominating and appointing, though he must obtain the consent of the Senate. He is the agent; the Senate may prevent his acting, but cannot act themselves.[29].

As a consequence it was maintained that, by their own arguments, those who contended for removal as incident to appointment must admit that the President, as the appointing agent, possessed the power of removal.

Having stated the constitutional arguments, it is next in order to determine the position of the former members of the Convention. As originally phrased, the bill provided that the respective secretaries should be removable by the President. This was ambiguous, being susceptible of the interpretation of being either a legislative grant of power or a legislative interpretation of the Constitution. Consequently, when the bill was under discussion, Representative Benson gave notice that he would move to amend the clause providing that the chief clerk should take charge of the office whenever a vacancy occurred so that it would read " when-

---

[28] Ibid., vol. i, p. 637.
[29] Ibid., vol. i, p. 561. Cf. Boudinot, p. 548; Sedgewick, p. 565.

ever the said principal officer shall be removed from office by the President of the United States, or in any other case of vacancy," with a view to striking out the ambiguous clause "to be removable by the President." [30]

This was excellent tactics. By moving the amendment while the original clause was in the bill, a way was left open for the proponents of the legislative grant idea to support the amendment without formal abandonment of their position. When the move to strike out was made the opponents of the whole idea would be in a dilemma. If they voted no, they retained the legislative grant clause to which they were opposed; if they voted aye, they left the added clause which made the whole bill only a legislative interpretation of a constitutionally granted power. The final vote on the completed bill would be, however, a clear-cut test of strength. Those opposed to it would be in favor of enhancing the importance of the Senate as an executive body; those voting aye would go on record as supporting the position that the Constitution granted the power.

By means of these votes we are able to classify the members of the House in three groups with almost entire accuracy. Fifteen members, including Madison, Clymer and Baldwin, voted aye on all three motions. They are consequently to be classed as out and out "constitutional grant" men. Fifteen voted no on the motion to strike out, after voting aye on the amendment. These included Carroll, Fitzsimons and Gilman. Not all perhaps were governed in their vote by the belief that the power was subject to legislative grant,[31] but it is reasonable to assume that such was the case with most. On the final vote on the bill, twenty-nine votes were cast for it, which included all six of the above-mentioned Convention members. In the twenty-two opposing votes there were only two Convention members, including Sherman and Gerry, the former, it will be remembered, one

---

[30] Annals, vol. i, p. 525.
[31] See Boudinot's explanation of his vote, Annals, vol. i, p. 606.

of the leaders of the weak executive forces in Philadelphia, the latter a "Grumbletonian." [32]

It remained to be seen, however, whether the Senate would divest itself of such important powers and by so doing consent to reduce its own importance in the constitutional scheme. The bill as it came to them presented a clear-cut issue, for all possibility that the idea of a legislative grant might be read into it was eliminated. It will again be of especial interest to see how the former members of the Convention, in this case exactly fifty per cent of the total membership, gave their voice.

The exact constitutional significance of the step which was about to be taken by the Senate was given clear enough expression on the floor. The notes of Ellsworth's speeches, taken by John Adams, show that he completely accepted the position taken by Madison. The notes read:

> There is an explicit grant to the President which contains the power of removal. The executive power is granted; not the executive powers hereinafter enumerated and explained. The President, not the Senate, appoint; they only consent and advise. The Senate is not an executive council; has no executive power. The grant to the President express not by implication. The powers of this Constitution are all vested; parted from the people, from the States, and vested, not in Congress, but in the President.
> The word sovereignty is introduced without determinate ideas. [This in reference to Butler's statement that the President was not sovereign, but either the United States, the people or Congress.] Power in the last resort. In this sense the sovereign executive is in the President.[33]

Maclay confirms Adams. He quotes Ellsworth as saying:

> I buy a square acre of land. I buy the trees, waters, and everything belonging to it. The executive power belongs to the President. The removing of officers is a tree on this acre. The power of removing is, therefore his. It is in him. It is nowhere else.

Also he "lamented the want of power in the President: Asked did *we ever quarrel* with the power of the Crown of Great Britain? No; we contended with the power of the Parliament. No one ever thought the power of the Crown

---

[32] So characterized by a correspondent of Jefferson's. Farrand, Records, vol. iii, p. 104.
[33] John Adams, Works, vol. iii, p. 409.

too great. Said he was growing infirm—should die, and should not see it—but the Government would fail, for want of power in the President." [34]

Paterson, too, adopted the same view. Adams' notes on his speech are:

> The executive coextensive with the legislative. Had the clause stood alone, would there not have been a devolution of all executive power? Exceptions are to be construed strictly. This is an invariable rule. [35]

Maclay similarly reports:

> Mr. Patterson got up. For a long time you could not know what he would be at. After, however, he had warmed himself with his own discourse, as the Indians do with their war song, he said he was for the clause continuing. He had no sooner said so, than he assumed a bolder tone of voice—flew over to England—extolled the Government—wished, in the most unequivocal language, that our President had the same powers. Said let us take a second view of England—repeating nearly the same thing. Let us take a third view of it, said he. And he then abused the Parliament for having made themselves first triennial, and lastly systennial. Speaking of the constitution, he said expressly these words, speaking of the removing of officers: *There is not a word of removability in it.* His argument was that the executive held this, as a matter of course. [36]

Butler, Lee, Grayson, Johnson, and Maclay were the chief speakers in the opposition. Adams' notes of Johnson's speech read:

> Gentlemen convince themselves that it is best the President should have the power, and then study for arguments. Exceptions. Not a grant. Vested in the President would be void for uncertainty. Executive power is uncertain. Powers are moral, mechanical, material. Which of these powers? What executive power? [37]

Butler, who followed Ellsworth, declared that he had in-

---

[34] Maclay, Sketches of Debate in the First Senate (Harris ed.), p. 108. Maclay further reports: "He absolutely used the following expressions with regard to the President: '*It is sacrilege to touch an hair of his head* and we may as well lay the President's head on a block and strike it off with a blow.' The way he came to use these words was, after having asserted that removing from office was his privilege, we might as well do this as deprive him of it. He had sore eyes and a green silk over them. On pronouncing the last of the two sentences, he paused, put his handkerchief to his face, and either shed tears, or affected to do so." Ibid., p. 107.

[35] Adams, Works, vol. iii, p. 411.

[36] Maclay, Debates, p. 109.

[37] Adams, Works, vol. iii, p. 412.

tended to vote for the clause, "but the arguments of the honorable gentleman from Connecticut, in endeavoring to support the clause, had convinced him, in the clearest manner, that the clause was highly improper," [38] and drew an analogy to the power to make treaties which, he said, ought "to be gone over, clause by clause, by the President and Senate together, and modelled." [39]   Grayson protested that the President was not above the law, as Ellsworth claimed, but could be sued.   "The people," he said, "will not like 'the jurors of our lord, the President,' nor 'the peace of our lord, the President.'" [40]

Richard Henry Lee took a somewhat different view.   He could not "see responsibility in the President or the great officers of State," fortified as they were "by a masked battery of constructive powers."   "The executive [was] not punishable but by universal convulsion, as Charles I. . . . There is no responsibility in the President or ministry." [41] These brief jottings of Adams show plainly that Lee saw, partly at least, the true meaning of British responsibility. Accordingly it is no surprise to find that he submitted a formal motion, the substance of which was, Maclay tells us, "that the officer should be responsible," and adds, "It was lost, of course." [42]   Again an opportunity for ministerial government was offered, and again rejected, "of course."

There can, then, be no question that the matter of removal was voted upon by the Senate with a full knowledge of what it signified in all its aspects.   The issue was crystal clear, and the majority of former Convention members were found voting for the bill as it stood, the division being Read, Bassett, Ellsworth, Strong, Paterson and Morris against Butler, Langdon, Johnson and Few.   The significance of the vote is the greater when it is remembered that instances where a

---

[38] Maclay, Debates, p. 107.
[39] Adams, Works, vol. iii, p. 409.
[40] Ibid., vol. iii, pp. 409–410.
[41] Ibid., vol. iii, p. 410.
[42] Maclay, p. 112.

political body voluntarily deprives itself of power are very few in all the history of government.

Twelve of eighteen former members of the Convention thus took the position that the President was the head of all the administrative departments. The propriety of presidential superintendence and control, the right of the chief executive to act through the instrumentality of agents subject to his choice and direction was the basis of the position of all the twelve who voted for removal by the President alone.

Nor was it in this debate alone that this interpretation is made manifest. The failure of the original treasury bill to call the treasury department an executive one was promptly rectified in the act providing for the salaries of "the executive officers of government," first in the list of which was the secretary of the treasury.[43] Representative Vining's home department bill, which failed only for reasons of economy, provided that the secretary was "in general to do and attend to all such matters as he may be directed to do by the President." [44] The temporary bill for the postoffice department provided that that officer was "to be subject to the direction of the President of the United States in performing the duties of his office, and in forming contracts for the transportation of the mail." [45] In fact, the permanent bill failed of passage through the Senate's insistence that the determination of routes was an administrative rather than a legislative function.[46]

This does not exhaust the evidence, but, surely, enough is included to demonstrate the erroneousness of the commonly accepted explanation that the presidential control over administration is an accidental result of the possession of the power of removal. The exact reverse is the true explana-

---

[43] Statutes at Large, vol. i, p. 67.

[44] Annals, vol. i, p. 692.

[45] Stat. L., vol. i, p. 70. This phrase was omitted from the permanent bill of 1792, but much water had run under the bridges by the time it was adopted.

[46] See Sherman's speech, Annals, vol. ii, p. 1937, and the whole debate, passim.

tion. The power of removal was rather derived from the general executive power of administrative control. The latter power has not been an extra-constitutional growth. It was the conscious creation of the men who made the Constitution. The President has possessed it as a constitutional power from the beginning of government under the Constitution.[47]

Similarly, the twelve former members of the Convention, and the majority, of the Congress, proceeded on the basis of the conviction that the participation of the Senate in executive business was a bad thing, and consequently to be reduced to a minimum. Even though all did not reach this conclusion by the same process of reasoning, the result is the same. The general principle was established, so far as possible, that, to use Madison's summary, "the Senate is associated with the President by way of exception, and cannot, therefore, claim beyond the exception," [48] and, as Paterson had said in the Senate, exceptions should be interpreted strictly.

With respect to senatorial participation in appointment, this interpretation reduced the Senate from a special administrative council, as some conceived it, to a participant in the exercise of the power of appointment, and that only as a purely negative check. With respect to senatorial participation in the appointment of ambassadors, the same is true. Instead of being a council for advising the President in the control of foreign affairs, waiving for the time the question of treaties, it was to possess merely a power to prevent bad appointments to diplomatic offices.

The fact that there was a strong minority who thought otherwise, who concluded, with Stone, that the Senate had "an immediate concern in and control over this business" of foreign affairs only serves to bring out the critical nature of

[47] With the exception, of course, of the period of the "tenure of office" act.

[48] Madison to Randolph, June 12, 1789; Works (Cong. ed.), vol. i, p. 476. Randolph, to Madison's surprise, approved this argument (ibid. to ibid., July 15, 1789; Works, Cong. ed., vol. i, p. 488) and may be included in the majority, making it 13 to 6.

the decision. The majority saw the aims of the minority and checked them. It was the view of Madison and not of Bland that prevailed.

The recognition that the President is the sole constitutional representative of the Union in its foreign relations is made even plainer by the terms of the foreign department bill. There was a real distinction made between this and the war department, on the one hand, and the treasury department on the other. But it consists not in any difference of super-intending power of the President, as is generally stated, but in the fact that the treasury department alone was created solely for the purpose of carrying out enactments of Con-gress. In all things concerning money the legal " impulse to action " had, from the nature of things, to come from Con-gress. This was only partly true of the war department, and not at all true of the foreign department. The sole purpose of that organization was to carry out, not legislative orders, as expressed in appropriation acts, but the will of the execu-tive. In all cases the President could direct and control, but in the " presidential " departments he could determine what should be done, as well as to how it should be done.[49]

That Congress recognized the difference appears from the fact that, in the case of the treasury department, the duties of the secretary were completely defined by law. Since the President could remove the officer, he could control him in the exercise of any discretion that was vested in him. He could not, however, direct him to disobey a law. But in the case of the foreign department, Congress was extremely care-ful to see to it that their power of organizing the department did not take the form of ordering the secretary what he should or should not do.

The whole question of the secretary's powers was left to the President, and the way left open for the " impulse to

---

[49] Sherman's remarks on giving the secretary of the treasury power to prepare revenue plans, while no similar power was con-ferred on the other secretaries. Annals, vol. i, pp. 630–631.

action" to come solely from that source. He was not to do certain things laid down by Congress, but:

> To perform and execute such duties as shall, from time to time, be enjoined on or intrusted to him by the President of the United States; agreeable to the Constitution, relative to correspondences, commissions, or instructions, to or with public ministers or consuls from the United States, or to negotiations with public ministers, or other foreigners, or to memorials or other applications from foreign public ministers, or other foreigners, or to such other matters respecting foreign affairs as the President . . . shall assign to the said department.[50]

Congress would indicate the field of the secretary's activities, but it would not go further. In the vivid phrase of Representative Sedgewick, the officer was to be "as much an instrument in the hands of the President, as the pen is the instrument of the Secretary in corresponding with foreign courts."[51]

Correspondence, instructions, in short, the transaction of foreign business, was thus recognized as a purely executive function. It belonged to the President by virtue of the executive grant, by virtue of the principle of strict construction of exceptions from his executive power, by virtue of his control over the secretary through his power of removal and through the terms of the departmental organization. On every side care was taken to emphasize the exclusively executive quality of the whole field.

Thus, when the question of appropriating funds for the diplomatic service was reached, a lump sum of $40,000 was voted, the amount to be expended being left to the President alone, subject only to a fixed maximum for each grade. The minority objected seriously. Sherman, their spokesman, argued as follows:

> The establishment of every treaty requires the voice of the Senate, as does the appointment of every officer for conducting the business. These two objects are expressly provided for in the Constitution, and they lead me to believe that the two bodies ought to act jointly in every transaction which respects the business of negotiation with foreign powers.[52]

---

[50] Stat. L., vol. i, p. 28.

[51] Annals, vol. i, p. 542.

[52] Sherman, Annals, vol. i, p. 1122. Cf. Stone, p. 1120, to the same effect.

But the majority turned its back on these arguments, and, by allowing the President to exercise this discretion alone, indicated again its purpose to pare the executive powers of the Senate to the irreducible minimum.

Even Jefferson accepted the prevailing doctrine without objection. In answer to a request from Washington for an opinion on the right of the Senate to negative the grade of a diplomatic appointee, he replied as follows:

> The Constitution has divided the powers of government into three branches. . . . It has declared that "the executive powers shall be vested in the President," submitting only special articles of it to a negative by the senate. . . . The transaction of business with foreign nations is executive altogether; it belongs, then, to the head of that department, *except* as to such portions of it as are specially submitted to the senate. *Exceptions* are to be construed strictly.[53]

Manifestly these arguments for a strict construction of Senatorial participation have a definite bearing on the question of the relations of the executive and the Senate in the business of making treaties, and especially on the point as to whether, as claimed by Senator Lodge, "the 'advice and consent' of the Senate are . . . coextensive with the 'power' conferred on the President, which is 'to make treaties' and apply to the entire process of treaty-making,"[54] an interpretation that is certainly strongly suggested by the words of the article.

There is much to support this view. The Federalist spoke of the power as being as much legislative as executive.[55] After the compromise had been submitted to the Convention, Morris still spoke of the Senate's power to make treaties.[56] Also the objection to the addition of the House as a ratifying

---

[53] Jefferson, Writings (Ford ed.), vol. v, p. 161.
[54] H. C. Lodge, "The Treaty Making Powers of the Senate," in A Fighting Frigate and other Essays and Addresses, pp. 231–232. Cited in R. Hayden, The Senate and Treaties, 1789–1817, p. 17. Dr. Hayden's exhaustive and scholarly treatment of the practice of Washington in making treaties makes it unnecessary for the present study to enter that field. It is believed, however, that in order to obtain a complete view of the question this anti-senatorial feeling should be taken into account.
[55] Federalist, No. 75 (Lodge ed.), p. 466.
[56] Farrand, Records, vol. ii, p. 523.

agent was partly due to a feeling that the plenipotentiary's act bound the sovereign, a fact strongly suggesting that it was regarded as wise to have the ratifying agent participate in the formulation of instructions.[57]   Even more significant is the practice of Washington in seeking the active coöperation of the Senate in the preliminary work of making treaties at the outset of his administration.[58]

But it does not follow that this was a universally held view. Both Spaight and Davie in the North Carolina ratification convention expressly declared that the power was executive in its nature,[59] and the latter described the Senate's part in the process as "the power of making, or rather ratifying, treaties." Mason in the Virginia convention spoke of the possibility that a "partial treaty" might be negotiated by the President.[60]   Charles Cotesworth Pinckney described the compromise by saying that "it was agreed to give the President a power of proposing treaties . . . and to vest the Senate . . . with the power of agreeing or disagreeing to the terms proposed."[61]   Even Richard Henry Lee admitted in the Senate that "the greater part of [the] power of making treaties [was] in the President."[62]

It is easily seen, too, that the arguments that the Senate's participation in appointment was not in the nature of the action of a council at all, that, as Representative Benson expressed it, the President and Senate were "two distinct bodies, and can only give a simple affirmative or negative,"[63] or, as Senator Ellsworth said, the Senate was "not an executive body," applied *mutatis mutandis* to the power to make treaties as well as to make appointments, whatever be thought of the arguments.

---

[57] Ibid., vol. ii, pp. 392–393, and above, chap. v, note 37.
[58] See Hayden, Senate and Treaties, chaps, i–v, especially chaps. i–iii and p. 19.
[59] Farrand, Records, vol. ii, pp. 342, 348.
[60] Elliot, Debates, vol. iii, p. 499.
[61] Farrand, Records, vol. iii, p. 250.
[62] Adams, Works, vol. iv, p. 410.
[63] Annals, vol. i, p. 526.

The truth is that a majority of the members of the Convention whose judgment is obtainable showed a dislike for the whole idea of the Senate's special powers, and the clause, if correctly interpreted, must be interpreted in the light of this attitude.   Unwillingness to give the power to the President alone and still more the insistence of the small States on an equal voice determined the compromise.[64]   " The small states," said Davie, " would not consent to confederate without an equal voice in the formation of treaties.   This difficulty could not be got over.   It arose from the unalterable nature of things." [65]   But the Senate was looked at askance by the nationalists as representing the States, by the strong executive men as weakening that department, by the large state men as destroying their due influence, and by the anti-federalists as the stronghold of aristocracy.   As Baldwin said in the House, and without contradiction, " the mingling of the powers of the President and Senate was strongly opposed in the convention. . . . One gentleman called it a monstrous and unnatural connexion. . . . This objection was not confined to the walls of the convention; it has been the subject of newspaper declamation, and perhaps justly so. Ought not we, therefore, to be careful not to extend this unchaste connexion any further?" [66]

Only a few desired that the President possess the unhampered power to make treaties.   But it does not follow that these others desired to see the Senate transformed into an executive council.   It is this, we believe, that determined the ready acquiescence given by the Senate to presidential negotiation without prior consultation.[67]   Had Washington chosen to make the issue sooner, there can be little doubt that he would have succeeded in maintaining his position.

The last principle, but one of equal importance with the others, which this removal debate at least tended to establish

[64] Adams, Works, vol. iii, p. 409.
[65] Farrand, Records, vol. iii, p. 348.
[66] Annals, vol. i, pp. 578–579.
[67] Hayden, Senate and Treaties, p. 37.

was that the executive is not limited to the enumerated powers, and that the vesting clause is a grant of power. Opponents to Madison's interpretation were not slow to object that, if it were admitted that the President had powers neither specifically granted nor even deducible from those specifically granted, the way was opened for an extension of executive powers that might come to include even the prerogative powers.[68] Nor was this argument fairly met. And yet, it would seem, it might have been. Executive power is under a definite restriction, even if the vesting clause be considered a grant, and one of a severe character. The national government is one of restricted powers. The President may do nothing that the national government may not do. But where, by the terms of the Constitution, the national government is vested with control over a certain sphere of action, that portion of the field is the President's which is executive in character. Thus the Constitution makes the national government the sole organ for the conduct of foreign affairs. And yet the powers which are necessary for it to take this duty upon it are not all conferred by the Constitution—the power to recognize new governments or new States, to dismiss foreign ministers, even to conduct general negotiations. Since they are not enumerated, they are the President's as of constitutional right, being of an executive character.

Whether or not this line of reasoning be regarded as juristically sound, it was undoubtedly something of the sort that the men who made the Constitution had in mind when they spoke of the executive power. To interpret the presidency strictly in terms of the language of the enumerated powers can then result only in inadequate concept of what the office signified. At least, we must extend the concept to include the sole right to administrative headship and to the management of the business of foreign affairs. And, we believe, in the last should be included the right to negotiate treaties independently of the Senate.

---

[68] See Annals, vol. i, pp. 485, 505–506, 566–567.

CHAPTER VII

Conclusions

The completion of the work of the first session of Congress marks the completion of the period of constitutional creation. It marks as well the flood tide of that movement towards a strong executive which it has been the chief purpose of the present study to trace. Already Maclay was entering his murmurings against the "court party" in his diary, and shortly "Republicanism," as opposed to the "monarchic" tendencies of the Federalists, was to put an end to further extensions of presidential power. The making of the Constitution, in the strict sense, was done.

The nature of the executive department which it created requires but little further analysis, for it was, in the main, the Wilson plan that triumphed. With its essential elements we have become familiar. It was essentially an integral part of that wider concept of limited government which is the most distinctive contribution of American political thought and experience to the art of government. As such it was based on the primary assumption that governmental powers are derived from the people by virtue of the people's grant, the Constitution, and are held by the departments of government by equal tenure.

We have seen how it was only by slow degrees that the leaders in political life in America were brought to a point where they were willing to grant this doctrine full play in the organization of their executives, to abandon the concept that sovereignty and legislative power are identical, to deny that there is a preëminence of the department whose function is legislation as compared with the other two. But when Wilson wrote into the report of the committee of detail the sentence, "the executive power of the United States shall be vested in a single person," it marked the final abandonment of the concept of the omnipotence of the legislature, and the substitution therefor of the characteristically American doctrine of coördinate departments. The unrestrained legislature and the subordinate executive had had its day, and, so far as the United States were concerned, had "ceased to be."

With the abandonment of the idea of the supreme legislature went the concept of executive responsibility to the legislature, and in its place came that of the executive as representative of and responsible to the people. This was a fundamental idea, and from it were derived the subsidiary principles of executive unity and personal responsibility, principles demanded as well by the requirements of a good executive, "energy, secrecy and dispatch." Executive integration, too, followed as a natural consequence, and the elimination of the constitutional council of the chief magistrate. Also, that this responsibility of the chief magistrate might be real, there must be relatively short terms with unrestricted eligibility for reëlection.

This solution was, after all, but an adaptation of the principle of representation, properly safeguarded, to the problem in hand. "The American States enjoy the glory and the happiness of diffusing this vital principle throughout all the different divisions and departments of government," wrote Wilson. "Representation is the chain of communication between the people and those to whom they have committed the important charge of exercising the delegated powers necessary for the administration of public affairs. This chain may consist of one link, or more links than one, but it should always be sufficiently strong and discernible."[1] For weal or woe, it was on the rock of the representative principle that American constitutionalism was founded.

It is somewhat remarkable, indeed, that the electoral procedure set up by the Constitution should so soon have been regarded as the equivalent of popular election, that the position of the President as the one, great national representative

[1] Wilson, Works, vol. i, p. 389.

should have been so readily accepted. But neither the one idea nor the other is a modern innovation. Both were inherent parts of Wilson's concept. " The tenure of his office, it is true is not hereditary, nor is it for life: but still it is a tenure of the noblest kind," Wilson wrote. " By being the man of the people, he is invested; by continuing to be the man of the people, his investiture will be voluntarily, and cheerfully, and honorably renewed." [2]

"Another reason why the power of removal should be lodged with the President, rather than the Senate," argued Representative Hartley, " arises from this connexion with the people. The President is the representative of the people in a near and equal manner; he is the guardian of his country. The Senate are the representatives of the State legislatures." [3]

" Is anything more plain," asked Representative Scott, " than that the President, above all the officers of Government, both from the manner of his appointment, and the nature of his duties, is truly and justly denominated the man of the people? Is there any other person who represents so many of them as the President? He is elected by the voice of the people of the whole Union. . . . No man in the United States has their concurrent voice but him." [4]

Whence came this concept? If the question be one of the influences that made such an executive possible, the answer is clear. The fundamental influence was the catalogue of legislative misdeeds which Madison enumerated in his list of causes of the calling of the Convention. The independent executive derives from the same source as the clause concerning the sanctity of contracts, on the one hand, from the same source as Washington's military " dictatorship," and

---

[2] Ibid., vol. i, p. 400.
[3] Annals, vol. i, p. 500.
[4] Ibid., vol. i, p. 554. Cf. Laurence, Annals, vol. i, p. 504; Clymer, Annals, vol. i, p. 509. For an opposing view, see Gerry, Annals, vol. i, p. 557. The exposition of the idea of the President as representative of the whole people was not confined to the House. See, for example, Nicholas' remarks on the treaty making power in the Virginia convention, Elliot, vol. iii, p. 240.

Robert Morris's financial "dictatorship" on the other. The state legislatures' excesses and the incompetency of Congress as an administrative body produced the presidency, exactly as today in State after State the excesses of the same state legislatures and the incompetency of state administrative systems are transforming the state governor into a miniature President.

Other influences were contributory to the same end. The fact that the first President was to be Washington had an undoubted effect. When men spoke of the great national representative, of the guardian of the people, they were thinking in terms of the Father of His Country.

"Entre nous, I do [not] believe they [the executive powers] would have been so great," wrote Pierce Butler to England, "had not many of the members cast their eyes toward General Washington as President; and shaped their Ideas of the Powers to be given a President, by their opinions of his Virtue."[5]

The dogma of separation of powers and that of checks and balances, as preached by "the famous Montesquieu," whose name was on every man's tongue, and by "the learned Blackstone," whose book was, in Patrick Henry's phrase, "in every man's hand,"[6] conditioned political thought, as did their interpretations, or rather misinterpretations, of the British constitutional system. But, it is submitted, they were not the determining influences. Otherwise, their teachings would not have meant one thing in 1776, another in 1787.

Indeed, the doctrine of separation fared far harder at the hands of the Convention than one would suppose from the continual appeals made to it. The fact is, as has been so clearly pointed out by Mr. W. F. Willoughby, that there are

---

[5] P. Butler to W. Butler, May 5, 1788; Farrand, Records, vol. iii, p. 301.

[6] There were 81 subscribers to the original subscription edition of the Commentaries in Virginia alone (1774), William and Mary Quarterly, Second Series, vol. i, No. 3, p. 183. Burke declared in 1775, "I hear as many Blackstones are sold in America as in England" (C. H. Van Tyne, the Causes of the War of Independence, p. 343).

few governments which are characterized by a greater degree
of functional overlapping.   The argument that, for example,
the veto power is only "an auxiliary precaution in favor of
the maxim" of separation[7] does not change the fact of partial
fusion.[8]

It was in the complete personal separation of powers that
the doctrine found its real application, but even here it may
be doubted whether the theory was the controlling factor.
National experience had already forced the acceptance of the
principle as applied to the administrative departments in order to secure competent executive men and to relieve, even
if against its will, an overworked Congress.   In the state
governments, the desire to secure an external check on the
legislature seemed to demand the same thing; and, finally,
the knowledge that the ability of a Member of Parliament to
hold other office had been utilized again and again as an
instrument of corruption, a knowledge which had profoundly
shaken all faith in Parliament's corporate integrity, might
well alone have been decisive.

It was through the interpretation of the British constitutional system as a contrivance of checks, Lords against Commons and both against the Crown, that Montesquieu and
Blackstone had their greatest influence.   Men were taught
to think of government, in fact all political life, as a conflict
of opposing interests rather than as a matter of coöperation.
From the nature of things, however, this meant, when applied
to the American system, chiefly that a strong national executive was needed to counterbalance legislative predominance.
Neither theorist nor foreign model was needed to demonstrate that fact.

---

[7] Farrand, Records, vol. ii, p. 77.

[8] See, on this point, Federalist, no. 47, where Madison qualifies the
doctrine so as to make it mean but very little, so far as functional
distribution is concerned.   It is the New Hampshire doctrine that
he quotes with approval, that separation should be maintained "as
far as the nature of a free government will admit; or as is consistent
with that chain of connection that binds the whole fabric of the constitution in one indissoluble bond of unity and amity." (Lodge
ed., p. 303.)   Madison italicized the qualification.

The truth is that the Fathers used the theorists as sources from which to draw arguments rather than specific conclusions. The chief problem of distribution of functions and organization of government was to get a sufficiently strong executive. When the argument was concerned with the participation of the Senate in executive functions, the appeal was made to separation; when it was the question of the veto power, the doctrine of checks was put forward. This may be made clearer by contrasting the strict construction attitude adopted toward the Senate's executive powers with the latitudinarian view of the President's veto power.

That the executive could properly control the legislature, to a degree at least, was all but universally admitted, not only, as is often stated, as a mere matter of self defence, but in order to prevent the enactment of unwise policies. A few quotations will suffice to make this clear. Wilson said, in support of the council of revision:

> The Judiciary ought to have an opportunity of remonstrating agst projected encroachments on the people as well as on themselves. It had been said that the Judges, as expositors of the Laws would have an opportunity of defending their constitutional rights. There was weight in this observation; but the power of the Judges did not go far enough. Laws may be unjust, may be unwise, may be dangerous, may be destructive; and yet not be so unconstitutional as to justify the Judges in refusing to give them effect.[9]

To this Gorham objected that judges possessed no "peculiar knowledge of the mere policy of public measures." [10] Madison agreed with Wilson that judicial participation "would . . . be useful to the Community at large as an additional check agst. a pursuit of those unwise and unjust measures which constituted so great a portion of our calamities," [11] and wrote in 1788 that "the revisionary power is meant a check to precipitate, to unjust, and to unconstitutional laws." [12] Even so confirmed an opponent to executive

---

[9] Farrand, Records, vol. ii, p. 73.
[10] Ibid., vol. ii, p. 73.
[11] Ibid., vol. ii, p. 74.
[12] Madison to J. Brown, October, 1788, Works (Cong. ed.), vol. i, pp. 188–195.

strength as Mason " observed that the defence of the Executive was not the sole object of the Revisionary power. He expected even greater advantages from it. Notwithstanding the precautions taken in the Constitution of the Legislature, it would so much resemble that of the individual States, that it must be expected frequently to pass unjust and pernicious laws. The restraining power was therefore essentially necessary. It would have the effect not only of hindering the final passage of such laws; but would discourage demagogues from attempting to get them passed." [13]

The true purpose of the Constitution was well stated by Ellsworth, who, in arguing for ratification, explicitly declared :

> We allow the president both an influence, tho' strictly speaking not
> a legislative voice; and think such an influence must be salutary.
> In the president all the executive departments meet, and he will be
> a channel of communication between those who make and those who
> execute the laws. Many things look fair in theory which in practice
> are impossible. If lawmakers, in every instance, before their final
> degree had the opinion of those who are to execute them, it would
> prevent a thousand absurd ordinances, which are solemnly made,
> only to be repealed, and lessen the dignity of legislation.[14]

Even with respect to the President's positive power to initiate legislation, there is no reason to believe that the same liberal interpretations were not held by many. Washington exercised, without objection, not only the right to recommend legislation in his annual message, but to recommend special measures, accompanying them with detailed reports.[15]

The explanation of this lack of consistency is simple enough. What was feared was the " everything was being drawn into the legislative vortex," and that the executive department would not be strong enough to fulfil its proper functions. The main thing with the majority was to

---

[13] Farrand, Records, vol. ii, p. 78.

[14] Oliver Ellsworth, " The Landholder," in The Federalist and Other Constitutional Papers (E. H. Scott ed.), vol. ii, p. 578.

[15] It is difficult to refrain from the conclusion that the influence of Washington on legislation was not greater than that of most subsequent presidents. Space nor time suffices for a consideration of the question here.

strengthen the executive, whatever the argument. " I see and *politically feel* that that will be the weak branch of the Government," Madison wrote at the time of the removal debates.[16]

Against one interpretation of the influence of the misinterpretation of the British constitution a protest should be entered, namely, that which sees in it the factor which determined the final form which the American national executive took, and the powers which he was given. The most extreme statement of this is perhaps that of Sir Henry Maine. He wrote :

> It is tolerably clear that the mental operation through which the framers of the American Constitution passed was this : they took the King of Great Britain, went through his powers, and restrained them whenever they appeared to be excessive, or unsuited to the circumstances of the United States. . . . It was George III they took for their model. . . . The original of the President of the United States is manifestly a treaty-making king actively influencing the executive government. . . . The framers of the American Constitution took George III's view of the kingly power for granted. They give the whole of the executive government to the President, and they do not permit his ministers to have a seat or speech in either branch of the legislature.[17]

As to the influence of the British prerogative powers on the American concept of the content of executive power, as here stated, little objection can be made. The theoretical powers of the British Crown were, and remain, a very exhaustive catalogue. No executive power could well have been given that was not contained therein. We have seen that in the Senate debate on removal these powers were extolled as properly being executive, but, after all, it was the selective process which, as Maine admits and as we have seen, was the important thing. The executive obtained those powers which the legislature was found unfit to possess.

It is in that portion of the argument that seeks to find in

---

[16] Madison to E. Randolph, May 31, 1789, Works (Cong. ed.), vol. i, p. 473.

[17] Maine, Popular Government, pp. 211–214, quoted approvingly in Stevens, Sources of the American Constitution, pp. 175–176. For a complete presentation of this view see Stevens, Sources, chap. vi, and citations of Brice, Freeman and Bagehot.

a misunderstood kingship the reason for the personal rule of the President and the elimination of the ministry (and it is there that the characteristic feature of the presidency is found) that a fundamental mistake is committed. In the first place, there is by no means that complete ignorance of the actual operation of the British system that is sometimes assumed. Morris saw that the prime minister was the King, that control in Parliament made the prime minister. Madison spoke of "examples in which the appointment and removal of ministers have been found to be dictated by one or other of [the legislative houses]."[18] Even Mr. Jackson from distant Georgia knew that "the executive power falls to the ground in England, if it cannot be supported by the Parliament; therefore a high game of corruption is played, and a majority secured to the ministry by the introduction of placemen and pensioners," though he saw in an American "treasury bench" only "ministers to govern and direct the measures of the Legislature, and to support the influence of their master."[19]

Wilson, whose views have a peculiar interest, analyzed the matter at considerable length, as follows:

The British Throne is surrounded by counsellors. With regard to their authority a profound and mysterious silence is observed. One effect, we know, they produce, and we conceive it to be a very pernicious one. Between power and responsibility they interpose an impenetrable barrier. Who possesses the executive power? The king. When its baleful emanations fly over the land, who are responsible for this mischef? His ministers. Amidst their multitude, and the secrecy, with which business . . . is transacted, it will be often difficult to select the culprits; still more so, to punish them. . . .

Though the power of the king's counsellors is not, so far as I can discover, defined or described in the British constitution; yet their seats are certainly provided for some purpose, and filled with some effect. What is wanting in authority may be supplied by intrigue; and in the place of constitutional influence, may be substituted that subtle ascendency, which is acquired and preserved by dissembled obsequiousness. . . .

In the United States, our first executive magistrate is not onubilated behind the mysterious obscurity of counsellors. Power is communicated to him with liberality, though with ascertained limitations. To him the provident or improvident use of it is to be ascribed. . . .

[18] Annals, vol. i, p. 518.
[19] Ibid., vol. i, p. 506.

He is the dignified, but accountable magistrate of a free and great people.[20]

Now, in this there may be misinterpretation, but there is no evidence of imitation. The truth is, ministerial government was not functioning too smoothly at the end of the eighteenth century. The preceding decades had proved the heyday of corruption, and undoubtedly that executive leadership, whether of King or Cabinet, which, whatever has been the theory of ministerial responsibility, has always characterized the British system, found in the practice its chief support. George III had injected a further complication by actively controlling his ministers. Parliaments proved restive on occasions and ejected ministries, but it is equally true that while those ministers were in office they controlled Parliament. It was the very essence of their tenure.

The makers of the Constitution saw deeply enough into this to distrust the whole system. Only a clear-sighted observer like Morris saw the possibility of the development of executive weakness such as has characterized the French system. But many more saw that the executive when in power controlled through corruption and disliked the practice. As a consequence the British system was abandoned for the representative chief magistrate.

It was not because the British King in theory named the members of his council that American ministerial officers were regarded as mere assistants of the President. It was not because of a complete misapprehension of the relations of those councillors to the Parliament that it was provided that no member of either House of Congress should hold other office. It was because the framers of the Constitution had a new theory of executive responsibility, based on unity, integration, choice by, and complete responsibility to, the people. There was no need for the paraphernalia of ministerial responsibility when the people at regular intervals could pass judgment on their representative. This, and not imitation of George III's kingship, determined Wilson and, through him, the Convention in their determination to avoid any scheme in

---

[20] James Wilson, Works, vol. i, pp. 399–400.

which the germ of ministerial development might be, which led Morris to abandon his idea of responsible ministers, which made it a matter of course that Richard Henry Lee's motion for a responsible ministry was defeated in the Senate.

There is no need to cross the Atlantic to find a working model of the American presidency. That it was the New York governorship is evident enough. Wilson's and Madison's insistence on the council of revision idea clearly indicates their views of the high importance of the principles of the New York instrument. It afforded the only American example of government by a constitution actually controlling the departments of government and at the same time a completely independent and very energetic and active chief magistrate. It is no accident that the executive article so closely resembles the New York articles. George Clinton was the wrong man for the place, but the principles of constitutional construction by virtue of which he exercised power were none the less judged good, with the safeguard, it was believed, against getting such a man into national office. The potentialities for the right man to do good were not obscured by the anti-nationalism and popular party proclivities of the then incumbent. The manner of operation of the New York constitution was, we may well believe, that in which it was hoped the new national executive would function.

The American executive has well justified the claims put forward by Wilson for uniqueness. In a very real sense it has proved a governmental creation, differing from its predecessors and their derivatives in a most decisive fashion. There is opportunity then for a real claim for authorship. Primarily it belongs to the little group of men who determined the construction of the New York constitution, Jay and Gouverneur Morris and Robert Livingston, but to James Wilson belongs the credit of crystallizing the concept and laying it before the Convention. Gouverneur Morris was rather the floor leader of the strong executive forces, probably as shrewd and adroit a one as any cause has ever had, but Morris, as we have seen, came to a realization of the true meaning of Wilson's idea only after he had undertaken this leadership. The principle was Wilson's. So with Madison. The idea plainly enough did not originate with him. He followed where another led. His political support was invaluable, but no just claim for authorship can be made for him.

There is small need to point out that the history of the presidency reveals it as operating to a great degree as Wilson envisaged it. Congressional caucuses have striven to name the incumbents of the office. The upper chamber has attempted and succeeded in making the President for a time the thing that Wilson dreaded, "the minion of the Senate." Executive control of treaty negotiations has been denounced first by one minority, then by another. Weak men have occupied the office without the ability to support its great responsibility. But there have always come into office at critical times men who would utilize its powers fearlessly, independently, and with a full acceptance of responsibility, striving each to be the "man of the people," to serve as a mouthpiece for the national will, to be the guardian of those great national interests intrusted to him, the conduct of war, maybe, the management of foreign affairs, the honest conduct of administrative business. These men have kept the original spirit of the Constitution alive.

At the beginning of our governmental history, Adams wrote: "The office, by its legal authority, defined in the Constitution, has no equal in the world, excepting those only which are held by crowned heads; nor is the royal authority in all cases to be compared to it." [21] Today we would amend by striking out the exception, and adding a new one, the uncrowned king of Great Britain, the Prime Minister.

With the wisdom of this process we do not deal, but it may not be amiss to recall two facts: that never yet has the choice of the people put into office a corrupt President, and that the office as organized successfully has withstood and completely recovered from the violent direct assault of a hate-blinded Congress. This in itself is no slight tribute.

INDEX